The Venture Capital Industry in Europe

Palgrave Macmillan Studies in Banking and Financial Institutions

Series Editor: **Professor Philip Molyneux**

The Palgrave Macmillan Studies in Banking and Financial Institutions will be international in orientation and include studies of banking within particular countries or regions, and studies of particular themes such as Corporate Banking, Risk Management, Mergers and Acquisitions, etc. The books will be focused upon research and practice, and include up-to-date and innovative studies on contemporary topics in banking that will have global impact and influence.

Titles include:

Yener Altunbas, Blaise Gadanecz and Alper Kara
SYNDICATED LOANS
A Hybrid of Relationship Lending and Publicly Traded Debt

Santiago Carbó, Edward P.M.Gardener and Philip Molyneux
FINANCIAL EXCLUSION

Franco Fiordelisi and Philip Molyneux
SHAREHOLDER VALUE IN BANKING

Munawar Iqbal and Philip Molyneux
THIRTY YEARS OF ISLAMIC BANKING
History, Performance and Prospects

Philip Molyneux and Munawar Iqbal
BANKING AND FINANCIAL SYSTEMS IN THE ARAB WORLD

Andrea Schertler
THE VENTURE CAPITAL INDUSTRY IN EUROPE

Palgrave Macmillan Studies in Banking and Financial Institutions
Series Standing Order ISBN 1–4039–4872–0

You can receive future titles in this series as they are published by placing a standing order. Please contact your bookseller or, in case of difficulty, write to us at the address below with your name and address, the title of the series and the ISBN quoted above.

Customer Services Department, Macmillan Distribution Ltd, Houndmills, Basingstoke, Hampshire RG21 6XS, England

The Venture Capital Industry in Europe

Andrea Schertler

palgrave
macmillan

First published 2006 by
PALGRAVE MACMILLAN
Houndmills, Basingstoke, Hampshire RG21 6XS and
175 Fifth Avenue, New York, N. Y. 10010
Companies and representatives throughout the world

PALGRAVE MACMILLAN is the global academic imprint of the Palgrave Macmillan division of St. Martin's Press, LLC and of Palgrave Macmillan Ltd. Macmillan® is a registered trademark in the United States, United Kingdom and other countries. Palgrave is a registered trademark in the European Union and other countries.

ISBN-13: 978–1–4039–9667–1 hardback

This book is printed on paper suitable for recycling and made from fully managed and sustained forest sources. Logging, pulping and manufacturing processes are expected to conform to the environmental regulations of the country of origin.

A catalogue record for this book is available from the British Library.

Library of Congress Cataloging-in-Publication Data
Schertler, Andrea.
The venture capital industry in Europe / by Andrea Schertler.
p. cm. – (Palgrave Macmillan studies in banking and financial institutions)
Includes bibliographical references and index.
ISBN 1–4039–9667–9 (cloth)
1. Venture capital–Europe. 2. Finance–Europe. I Title. II. Series.

HG5422.S34 2006
332'.04154094–dc22

2005058649

10 9 8 7 6 5 4 3 2 1
15 14 13 12 11 10 09 08 07 06

Contents

List of Tables and Figure

Tables

Figure

List of Abbreviations

AFIC	Association Francaise des Investisseurs en Capital
AKES	Closed-end Venture Capital Mutual Fund
AVCJ	Asian Venture Capital Journal
BES	Business Investment Scheme
BTU	Beteiligungsprogramm für kleine Technologieunternehmen
BVK	Bundesverband Deutscher Kapitalbeteiligungsgesellschaften
CEPR	Centre for Economic Policy Research
EASDAQ	European Association of Securities Dealers Automated Quotation
EBAN	European Business Angel Network
EIS	Enterprise Investment Scheme
ERISA	Employee Retirement Income Security Act
EVCA	European Venture Capital Association
FCPI	Fonds Communs de Placement dans l'Innovation
FCPR	Fonds Communs de Placement à Risques
GDP	Gross Domestic Product
GMM	Generalized Method of Moments
IGIER	Innozenzo Gasparini Institute for Economic Research
IPO	Initial Public Offering
IRR	Internal Rate of Return
KfW	Kreditanstalt für Wiederaufbau
MBG	Mittelständische Beteiligungsgesellschaft
MSCI	Morgan Stanley Capital International
NASDAQ	National Association of Securities Dealers Automated Quotation System
NBER	National Bureau of Economic Research
NEGBIN	negative binomial
NVCA	National Venture Capital Association
OECD	Organisation for Economic Co-operation and Development
SBA	Small Business Administration
SBIC	Small Business Investment Company
SOFARIS	Société Francaise de Garantie des Financements des Petites et Moyennes Entreprises
UBBG	Gesetz über Unternehmensbeteiligungsgesellschaften
VAT	Value-Added Tax
VCT	Venture Capital Trust

Acknowledgements

The work presented in this book has benefited from many discussions with other researchers. Comments by Philip Molyneux of Bangor University and Peter Nippel of Kiel University improved the arguments and structures in this book. Moreover, Peter Nippel gave me an ongoing motivation. My particular thanks go also to the researchers involved in a former project on *European Integration, Financial Systems and Corporate Performance* that was funded by the European Commission. The discussions taking place therein substantially stimulated my thoughts about this field. Moreover, my thanks go to Tereza Tykvova of the Centre for European Economic Research, Josh Lerner of Harvard University and Antoinette Schoar of the MIT Sloan School of Management for stimulating discussions on internationalization in private equity markets.

I am indebted to those people who helped in collecting and transforming data. In particular, I am indebted to Kristina Kittelmann, Laura Krische and Heiko Rachinger for providing highly qualified data assistance.

Moreover, I would like to acknowledge the stimulating environment for conducting research at the Kiel Institute for World Economics. Part of this book was written while I was visiting the National Bureau of Economic Research (NBER). The hospitality and stimulating environment of the NBER is gratefully acknowledged.

I would also like to thank the people who turned the manuscript into a book. Karin Kristahl edited various versions of the text with great expertise. Paul Kramer did a wonderful final reading.

1
Introduction

The extraordinary success of several venture-capital-backed firms such as Apple, Federal Express, Intel and Microsoft has spurred academic and policy discussion on venture capital finance. The academic discussion has spurred knowledge creation about venture capital finance, while the policy discussion has centred on the role of venture capital finance as a prerequisite for productivity and employment growth. The role of venture capital finance in facilitating employment and productivity growth has made venture capital a major target of European governments' financial market policies. European governments have made a variety of attempts to facilitate young high-technology firms' access to equity capital by improving the regulatory conditions venture capital companies face and by granting rather generous subsidies.

In economic theory, venture capital finance is defined as the financial means offered temporarily in the form of equity or similar financing tools to young high-technology firms in combination with management support and monitoring services provided by a technologically experienced intermediary, the venture capital company. Venture capital companies' management support services in high-technology firms are at the heart of venture capital finance because entrepreneurs of high-technology firms are proficient in their own technology field but they lack the expertise to successfully build up corporate firms and commercialize newly developed products. Therefore, venture capital companies' management support services are assumed to add value to high-technology firms. Besides adding value that might improve the risk-return profile of the firms they finance, venture capital companies further improve the risk-return profile of their portfolios by specializing in particular industries and/or stages of firms' development, or by financing investment deals together with other venture capital companies.

Venture capital companies are not interested in building up a long-term portfolio. Rather, they aim at exiting from their portfolio firms after some time. They realize most of their returns when exiting from their portfolio firms. When they sell their shares in high-technology firms in an initial public offering, their investment is assumed to be an indication of the quality of the portfolio firm to other less informed investors. Because they aim at exiting successfully after some years from the participations they have in their portfolio firms, liquid exit channels, such as stock market segments for fast-growing firms, play a central role in the development of venture capital industries.

Managers of venture capital funds not only provide monitoring and management support services to the firms in their portfolios, but also raise funds from capital providers, such as pension funds and insurance companies. The investment interests of managers of venture capital funds are not necessarily identical with the investment interests of the capital providers. This divergence in investment interests leads to specially designed contracts between the venture capital companies and the capital providers. For example, managers of venture capital companies often invest alongside with capital providers in the funds they raise.

Empirically, it is not easy to identify whether a particular venture capital company provides monitoring and management support in addition to financial means. There are multitude reasons for this. First, venture capital companies have to be distinguished from other investment companies that may be specialized in management buy-out activities. Second, the quality of monitoring and support services cannot be measured directly. Available measures, such as the hours that venture capital companies spend with the firms in their portfolios, do not inform about the productivity and experience of the venture capital companies. However, information on the quality and intensity of monitoring and support services is needed to be able to empirically identify the theoretically modelled value that venture capital companies add to the firms in their portfolios.

Generally, data on venture capital investments as defined theoretically above are not available for European countries. Data are, however, available for the broader asset class 'private equity', which refers to both venture capital activity and management buy-out activity. Empirically, venture capital activity is often identified using the firms' development stages. Firms receiving capital in the early stage and/or in the expansion stage are classified as venture-capital-backed. The empirical identification of venture capital backing, however, ignores whether the venture capital company provides monitoring and management support services that potentially add value to young high-technology firms.

Aims of the book

This book has two aims. The first aim is to bring together many pieces of empirical evidence from European venture capital and private equity industries in order to paint a colourful picture of the *microeconomics of venture capital finance*. At the current stage of research on venture capital finance in Europe, combining many pieces of evidence is relevant for future research because research output has already reached a substantial amount and depth, but it has focused most often only on a few facets of venture capital finance, such as the investment behaviour of venture capital companies, while ignoring other aspects of venture capital finance, such as the fundraising behaviour of venture capital companies. Taking the interdependencies between investment behaviour and fundraising behaviour into account may, however, be necessary to test hypotheses adequately. In this book, the discussion of the microeconomics of venture capital finance includes a detailed discussion of the fundraising, investing and exiting behaviour of venture capital companies as well as a discussion of venture capital companies' portfolio and internationalization strategies.

The second aim of this book is to describe and discuss the *industry features of venture capital finance* for European countries. The first industry feature of venture capital finance concerns cross-country variations in venture capital and private equity investments in the light of differences in financial market designs and in regulation of entrepreneurial activity. The second industry feature concerns the allocation of venture capital investments across industries and its link to the development and creation of industries in European countries. The third industry feature concerns internationalization in the venture capital industry and its link to the general globalization of financial markets. In recent years, the venture capital industry has also become more globalized, which may change not only the size of the venture capital industry in particular countries but also the microeconomics of venture capital finance. By addressing and combining the microeconomics of venture capital finance and the industry features, this book will identify some of the limits of recent research, and will raise questions that should be answered by future research.

Overview

The book is divided into eight chapters. The following chapter presents country-level data on private equity investments and fundraising around the globe and discusses the tax and legal environments of the private equity industries in European countries. Data on venture capital activity defined as a combination of financial means and management support are not available. However, data on private equity investments that cover venture capital and management buy-out activities are available for a large number of countries and an impressive number of years. Private equity investments in the early stage of firms will serve as an approximation of venture capital investments. Due to the difficulties in distinguishing venture capital companies and management buy-out companies I most often use the term private equity companies to refer to both groups. I use the term venture capital company when referring to venture capital companies operating in the United States. Moreover, I use the term venture capital company when referring to theoretical arguments that cannot be applied directly to management buy-out companies.

Chapter 3 focuses on the fundraising behaviour of private equity companies. First, it discusses one important aspect of the European private equity industry, namely the heterogeneity of private equity companies as regards to various fundraising sources, such as capital providers, and investment sources, such as investment specialization in particular stages of firms' development. Then, it presents data on the relevance of various capital providers in European countries, followed by a description of the contractual relationship between private equity companies and their capital providers.

Chapter 4 focuses on the investment behaviour of private equity companies. First, it describes the characteristics of those firms most likely receiving private equity finance. Then, it discusses the adverse selection and moral hazard problems determining the way in which venture capital companies deal with the firms in their portfolios, followed by a discussion of the value that venture capital companies add to their portfolio firms. A discussion of the portfolio strategies of venture capital and private equity companies completes this chapter.

Chapter 5 deals with the exiting behaviour of private equity companies from the firms in their portfolios. First, it describes the relevance of various exit channels used by private equity companies. Then, it discusses the role of stock markets for developments in the private equity industries, followed by discussing the relevance of the grandstanding and certification hypotheses. A description of returns on private equity and venture capital investments, and on private equity funds, completes this chapter. Thus, the well-known venture capital cycle – fundraising, investing and exiting – (Gompers and Lerner 1999a) is at the focus of Chapter 3 to 5.

Chapter 6 deals with cross-country variations in venture capital and private equity investments. While Chapters 3 to 5 focus on both the microeconomics of venture capital finance and the industry features, this chapter focuses only on the industry features. However, it also uses the insights of the microeconomics of venture capital finance presented in the Chapters 3 to 5 in order to ascertain which factors are crucial to private equity investments at a country level. It first introduces the empirical method and describes the variables used in the empirical analysis. Then, estimation results are discussed. A discussion of the robustness of the estimation results yielded completes this chapter.

Chapter 7 deals with the link between industry specialization on a country level and the private equity investments available in a country. As Chapter 6, this chapter focuses only on the industry features of venture capital finance. First, it describes the comparative advantages of those industries in which venture capital and private equity companies often invest. Then, it discusses whether private equity finance can be a source of comparative advantage for the industries in which private equity companies prefer to invest.

Chapter 8 deals with internationalization strategies in private equity industries. This chapter adds to the microeconomics and also to the industry features of venture capital finance. First, it describes international private equity flows in Europe. Then, it discusses why private equity and venture capital companies might be interested in being internationalized even if the monitoring and supporting services are likely to be more effective if venture capital finance is regionally concentrated. Using data on private equity companies, and country-level data, this chapter provides some tentative results regarding internationalization in private equity industries.

Chapter 9 summarizes the main insights and addresses future research questions.

2
Private Equity Industries around the Globe

This chapter deals with private equity and venture capital industries around the globe. The first venture capital company in the world was established in the United States in the mid-1940s. In some European countries, private equity industries came into existence in the early 1980s, in other European countries private equity industries were non-existent until the end of the 1990s. In recent years, private equity industries in several Asian countries have gained momentum.

The first part of this chapter describes recent developments in terms of fundraising and private equity investments in European and non-European countries. The second part discusses the tax and legal environments of capital providers, high-technology firms and private equity companies that help in explaining and understanding differences in private equity industries across countries.

Recent developments

The size of the private equity industries varies substantially across countries and over time. In the following, I discuss first the size of the private equity industries in 2003, and then the intensity of the upswing that took place at the end of the 1990s.

Size of the industries in 2003

Table 2.1 gives the amounts of new funds that private equity companies have raised for their private equity investments from capital providers, such as banks, insurance companies and pension funds. Because the countries under consideration differ substantially in size, I have scaled new funds raised by the countries' gross domestic product (GDP). In the

United States, new funds raised for private equity investments accounted for more than 23 per mille of GDP, followed by the United Kingdom and Sweden, whose new funds raised accounted, however, for only about 9 and 8 per mille of GDP in 2003. In many European countries, such as Austria, Belgium and Germany, new funds raised accounted for even less than 1 per mille of GDP in 2003. Thus, in terms of fundraising for private equity investments, the private equity industry in the United States is by far the largest industry in the world.

From an economic point of view, private equity investments are more informative than new funds raised for private equity investments, since the latter do not necessarily result in investments in the respective year. Therefore, Table 2.2 gives the amounts that private equity companies invested in portfolio firms for the European, and selected Asian countries for the years 1991 to 2003. For the United States, the table reports the amounts that venture capital companies invested in portfolio firms, excluding investments in firms' later stages of development. Because of the different definitions, US investments as per mille of GDP were substantially lower compared to new funds raised for private equity investments.

According to the data presented in Panel (a) in Table 2.2, the private equity industries in the United Kingdom, Finland and Sweden are substantially larger than in other European countries. Private equity industries in other European countries are negligible given the size of these countries.

Comparing new funds raised and private equity investments indicates that some countries, such as the United Kingdom, were more successful in raising new funds than in investing private equity. One reason for this might be that the United Kingdom is a financial centre that generally attracts substantial amounts of foreign capital. The language, the market-based financial system and its integration in the world's financial markets may explain these amounts of foreign capital. Another reason might be that regulation of private equity funds, and investment incentives, such as capital gains taxes, are more favourable in the United Kingdom than in other countries. I will come back to this below.

Some of the Asian countries were rather successful in realizing large amounts of private equity investments, as Panel(b) in Table 2.2 indicates. In 2003, private equity investments in Bangladesh accounted for more than 8 per mille of GDP. In other countries, such as Singapore and Korea, private equity investments accounted for 6 and 4.7 per mille of GDP, respectively. In Australia, private equity investments accounted for almost 6 per cent of GDP.

Table 2.1 New funds raised around the globe
This table reports new funds raised by private equity companies as per mille of GDP.

	1991	1992	1993	1994	1995	1996	1997	1998	1999	2000	2001	2002	2003
Austria	0.000	0.000	0.000	0.000	0.007	0.137	0.331	0.637	0.915	1.115	0.638	0.801	0.726
Belgium	0.532	0.454	0.552	0.460	0.789	0.897	0.878	1.837	3.272	3.259	2.561	0.479	0.787
Denmark	0.233	0.090	0.116	0.865	0.203	0.007	0.016	0.297	1.043	4.968	2.777	1.646	1.122
Finland	0.121	0.041	0.122	0.450	0.549	0.459	2.155	3.137	5.234	4.377	3.004	5.149	1.052
France	1.122	0.787	0.759	0.924	0.669	0.866	0.864	2.915	3.159	5.262	3.721	0.302	1.308
Germany	0.551	0.516	0.126	0.171	0.117	0.186	1.383	0.971	2.340	3.012	1.790	0.780	0.560
Greece	0.198	0.211	na	na	0.186	0.275	0.579	0.664	0.724	2.518	0.381	0.464	0.188
Ireland	1.050	1.133	0.690	3.967	0.236	0.334	0.436	2.116	3.537	1.918	1.821	1.574	0.445
Italy	0.300	0.563	0.380	0.369	0.285	0.740	1.048	0.872	1.584	2.505	1.539	1.583	1.487
Netherlands	0.420	0.341	0.488	0.899	0.847	4.436	2.584	3.284	2.827	6.940	1.667	2.684	4.517
Norway	0.348	0.126	0.641	0.367	0.404	0.751	0.558	3.305	0.992	2.746	1.929	1.713	1.625
Portugal	0.206	0.271	1.299	1.534	1.055	0.421	0.562	0.463	0.658	1.313	0.961	0.561	0.959
Spain	0.435	0.491	0.519	0.148	0.323	0.119	0.828	1.309	1.114	3.135	1.149	0.916	1.180
Sweden	0.527	1.598	0.737	1.307	2.308	0.236	4.512	4.519	4.200	13.960	7.410	2.504	8.043
Switzerland	0.107	0.227	0.320	0.239	0.199	0.657	0.326	0.923	2.414	3.693	2.386	0.711	1.232
United Kingdom	1.568	1.509	1.507	4.407	2.122	3.985	10.462	7.058	7.201	11.323	12.811	8.551	9.436
United States	4.840	4.633	4.602	4.991	5.461	6.161	7.605	10.384	16.066	23.249	25.365	24.648	23.403

Source: EVCA (various issues), NVCA (2004) and IMF (2003), own calculations.

Table 2.2 Private equity investments around the globe

This table reports private equity investments as per mille of GDP. For the United States, this table reports the amounts that venture capital companies invested in portfolio firms.

Panel (a)

	1991	1992	1993	1994	1995	1996	1997	1998	1999	2000	2001	2002	2003
Austria	0.022	0.005	0.003	0.001	0.006	0.005	0.101	0.261	0.446	0.775	0.683	0.661	0.501
Belgium	0.608	0.789	0.500	0.548	0.550	0.527	0.826	1.147	2.855	2.281	1.611	1.378	1.129
Denmark	0.201	0.109	0.131	0.143	0.223	0.236	0.149	0.259	0.714	1.595	1.864	1.321	2.201
Finland	0.259	0.195	0.240	0.274	0.352	0.392	1.058	1.622	2.071	2.952	1.895	3.262	3.088
France	0.936	0.888	0.822	0.953	0.718	0.729	1.000	1.359	2.080	3.731	2.227	3.829	2.724
Germany	0.387	0.391	0.380	0.463	0.369	0.391	0.712	1.009	1.597	2.348	2.138	1.189	1.166
Greece	0.033	0.208	na	na	0.103	0.366	0.168	0.184	0.633	1.609	0.783	0.321	0.168
Ireland	0.943	0.643	0.510	0.577	0.366	0.646	0.542	0.824	1.174	2.169	1.253	0.822	1.894
Italy	0.683	0.648	0.321	0.319	0.274	0.519	0.590	0.869	1.606	2.543	1.793	2.083	2.330
Netherlands	1.135	0.894	0.757	1.124	1.537	1.878	2.285	2.992	4.572	4.764	4.396	3.869	2.404
Norway	0.489	0.238	0.423	0.607	1.058	0.665	1.225	1.236	1.786	1.635	1.469	0.990	1.413
Portugal	0.725	0.669	1.113	0.963	0.671	0.396	0.679	0.490	1.098	1.585	0.884	0.533	0.893
Spain	0.459	0.346	0.294	0.287	0.370	0.415	0.533	0.688	1.278	1.846	1.833	1.386	1.795
Sweden	0.235	0.237	0.341	1.014	0.450	1.970	1.609	0.916	5.417	8.848	8.341	5.728	3.797
Switzerland	0.180	0.335	0.238	0.341	0.201	0.531	0.238	0.896	1.769	2.348	0.870	1.063	0.782
United Kingdom	2.058	2.211	1.981	2.597	3.035	3.169	3.783	5.597	8.391	8.450	4.331	6.102	8.522
United States	0.381	0.567	0.582	0.594	1.039	1.483	1.823	2.454	5.926	10.828	4.052	2.024	1.643

Source: EVCA (various issues), NVCA (2004) and IMF (2003), own calculations.

Table 2.2 Private equity investments around the globe – *continued*
This table reports private equity investments as per mille of GDP. For the United States, this table reports the amounts that venture capital companies invested in portfolio firms.

	Panel (b)	
	2002	2003
Australia	3.030	5.732
Bangladesh	na	8.454
China	0.268	1.135
Hong Kong	4.687	0.932
India	2.073	1.459
Indonesia	3.219	3.124
Japan	0.597	1.672
Korea	3.558	4.667
Malaysia	0.336	0.289
New Zealand	0.417	0.850
Philippines	0.013	0.819
Singapore	4.768	5.933
Sri Lanka	na	0.548
Thailand	0.552	0.322

Source: AVCJ (2005), and IMF (2003), own calculations.

Upswing in the 1990s

New funds raised for private equity investments increased substantially at the end of the 1990s and dropped sharply after the stock market bubble burst in the information and communications industry in 2000. In the United States, new funds raised for private equity investments increased from about $5 billion at the beginning of the 1990s to more than $100 billion in 2000 before it dropped to about $10 billion in 2002 and 2003 (NVCA 2004). European venture capital markets lagged behind the development in the United States by six to 12 months (Smith 2004a). In Europe, new funds raised for private equity investments increased from about €5 billion at the beginning of the 1990s to about €48 billion in 2000, and then dropped to €38 billion in 2001 (EVCA various issues).[1] In Asia, new funds raised for private equity investments increased from about $5 million in 1994 to about $18 million in 2000, before it dropped to $10 million in 2001 (AVCJ 2005).

In the United States, the upswing of the 1990s in venture capital investments started in 1994. As the data in Table 2.2 indicate, venture capital investments as per mille of GDP increased from 0.6 in 1994 to

1.5 in 1996. However, this increase was rather moderate compared to the increase at the end of the 1990s. Venture capital investments as per mille of GDP rose from 2.5 in 1998 to 5.9 in 1999 and reached a peak of 10.8 in 2000. Venture capital investments dropped sharply after the stock market bubble burst in 2000. In 2001 and 2002, they accounted only for 4.1 and 2.0, respectively. In 2003, they accounted only for about 1.6 per mille of GDP, which is very low compared to the investments in 2000 but high compared to the investments at the beginning of the 1990s.

The upswing in the European private equity industries took place later than in the US venture capital industry. The European industries started to grow between 1996 and 1997, during which time private equity investments increased by more than 40 per cent to about €10 billion. After that, investments increased substantially until 2000. However, the growth rate of private equity investments between 1998 and 2000 was lower than the respective growth rate of US venture capital investments.

During the boom at the end of the 1990s, many US venture capital companies opened offices in Europe and directed funds to European countries. There were several reasons for them to enter European markets, such as geographical diversification, and avoiding the strong deal competition in the United States. This inflow of foreign companies changed the European model from being based mainly on strong financial background towards acknowledging operational expertise in financing high-technology firms (Hardymon *et al.* 2003). US companies entered the European markets by recruiting staff from existing European private equity companies, by transplanting employees from the United States, or by setting up partnerships with local companies (Hardymon *et al.* 2003). After the stock market bubble burst however, many US venture capital companies closed their European offices (Hardymon *et al.* 2003).

Table 2.2 indicates the distribution of private equity investments across European countries is unequal. Some countries such as United Kingdom and Sweden have relatively high private equity investments, while other countries, such as Greece and Austria, have relatively few private equity investments given their country size. In addition, country groups such as the Scandinavian countries are rather heterogeneous. Hyytinen and Pajarinen (2003) have documented that private equity investments in Denmark, Finland and Norway, relative to their GDPs, are below the European average, while private equity investments in Sweden are above the European average.

The dynamics in European private equity industries during the 1990s also differed substantially. Some countries realized extraordinary growth rates in private equity investments. Private equity investments in Austria, for example, increased from 0.02 per mille of GDP in 1991 to 0.7 in 2001. By contrast, private equity investments in the United Kingdom increased from 2.1 per mille of GDP in 1991 to 8.5 in 2000. These differences in the dynamics of private equity investments suggest that private equity industries in European countries are in various development stages; some European countries already have relatively established private equity industries, while other countries may be in the process of developing such industries.

The fundraising and investment data presented in Tables 2.1 and 2.2 show a very interesting facet of private equity industries: private equity activity is highly volatile and seems to move with developments in stock markets. When stock market performance improves, private equity companies may have higher incentives to invest in high-technology firms, and they may be able to raise new funds from capital providers more easily. The recent literature has analysed the link between stock market performance and the fundraising of private equity companies. For the United States, Gompers and Lerner (1998) found that the previous years' equity value of venture-capital-backed firms when going public affects fundraising positively. US venture capital companies that have industry experience in financing high-technology firms increase their investments more than their less experienced counterparts when stock market performance improves (Gompers *et al.* 2005). Moreover, for the United States, Bouis (2003) has documented a positive relationship between fundraising and the level of lagged proceed-weighted initial returns in stock markets.

Private equity investments cover different types of investments. More specifically, private equity investments cover investments in firms that are in the early stage of development, in which investment risks are very high, and in firms that require capital in order to finance, for example, a management buy-out or buy-in. The early stage of a firm begins when it is forming its initial business concept and may end when it launches its initial marketing campaign. With management buy-outs, capital is required to enable current operating management teams or investors to acquire a whole or a significant part of the firm (EVCA 2002). With management buy-ins, capital is required to enable a management team from outside the firm to acquire a whole or a significant part of the firm (EVCA 2002). In empirical research, private equity investments in the early stage of development are often used as

Table 2.3 Early-stage investments in Europe and the United States
This table reports private equity investments in the early stage as per mille of GDP. For the United States, this table reports venture capital investments in the early stage as per mille of GDP.

	1991	1992	1993	1994	1995	1996	1997	1998	1999	2000	2001	2002	2003
Austria	0.005	0.000	0.001	0.000	0.002	0.001	0.016	0.064	0.071	0.286	0.192	0.124	0.131
Belgium	0.153	0.077	0.062	0.076	0.032	0.099	0.138	0.619	0.896	1.069	0.390	0.417	0.140
Denmark	0.049	0.009	0.030	0.031	0.025	0.016	0.019	0.085	0.189	0.198	0.853	0.752	0.496
Finland	0.113	0.077	0.076	0.064	0.082	0.088	0.082	0.531	0.565	1.041	1.036	0.706	0.592
France	0.029	0.037	0.014	0.022	0.022	0.083	0.072	0.197	0.383	0.812	0.381	0.262	0.253
Germany	0.027	0.029	0.032	0.047	0.049	0.052	0.108	0.241	0.502	0.814	0.557	0.266	0.137
Greece	na	na	na	na	0.040	0.071	0.052	0.041	0.177	0.736	0.237	0.092	0.075
Ireland	0.123	0.033	0.080	0.053	0.017	0.052	0.020	0.266	0.453	1.084	0.326	0.214	0.244
Italy	0.078	0.072	0.007	0.043	0.048	0.046	0.072	0.137	0.133	0.462	0.239	0.051	0.045
Netherlands	0.079	0.071	0.076	0.146	0.251	0.291	0.457	0.480	0.914	0.926	0.428	0.452	0.079
Norway	0.026	0.021	0.079	0.128	0.047	0.045	0.026	0.093	0.205	0.575	0.345	0.361	0.284
Portugal	0.121	0.091	0.066	0.092	0.052	0.013	0.120	0.129	0.078	0.266	0.131	0.080	0.428
Spain	0.109	0.081	0.041	0.026	0.040	0.025	0.043	0.089	0.164	0.328	0.170	0.152	0.075
Sweden	0.007	0.005	0.011	0.010	0.032	0.026	0.021	0.110	1.024	0.876	0.973	0.972	0.641
Switzerland	0.013	0.002	0.016	0.030	0.003	0.022	0.009	0.271	0.817	0.218	0.267	0.448	0.313
United Kingdom	0.081	0.064	0.056	0.066	0.032	0.044	0.085	0.140	0.186	1.034	0.581	0.360	0.391
United States	0.135	0.180	0.203	0.229	0.421	0.562	0.584	0.836	1.662	2.982	0.989	0.418	0.332

Source: EVCA (various issues), NVCA (2004), and IMF (2003), own calculations.

an approximation of venture capital activity (Jeng and Wells 2000, Da Rin *et al.* 2004). Therefore, Table 2.3 gives early-stage investments as per mille of GDP for European countries and the United States.

The European countries differed considerably with respect to investments in the early stage of firms' development, even though they all experienced an increase in investments during the 1990s. In 2003 and relative to GDP, early-stage investments were highest in Sweden, Denmark and Finland, while in Greece, Italy, the Netherlands and Spain early-stage investments hardly played a role.

Table 2.3 shows another interesting point to be mentioned. Early-stage investments in the United States as per mille of GDP were *per se* not always substantially higher than in the European countries. There were several countries and several years in which early-stage investments in European countries were at least as high as the investments in the United States. For example, in 1991, early-stage investments accounted for 0.13 per mille of GDP in the United States compared to 0.15 per mille of GDP in Belgium. In 2001, early-stage investments accounted for 0.99 per mille of GDP in the United States compared to 1.04 per mille of GDP in Finland.

The tax and legal environments

The tax and legal environments in the European countries are often mentioned as one explanation for the differences in the private equity investments and early-stage investments across European countries. The tax and legal environments do not only affect capital providers' supply of new funds, and portfolio firms' demand for private equity. They also affect the investment behaviour of private equity companies. However, the aspects of the tax and legal environments relevant for the private equity industries are too complex to be described in detail here. Nevertheless a short, and often incomplete description of certain aspects of the tax and legal environments will be presented in the following.

In its *Benchmarking Report on European Tax and Legal Environments* of 1 February 2004, the European Venture Capital Association (EVCA)[2] provides information on several pieces of regulations and constructs a single index of whether the tax and legal environments are favourable for the development of private equity industries in European countries. According to this single index, the United Kingdom and Ireland have the most favourable environments for developing large private equity industries, followed by Greece, the Netherlands, Portugal and Belgium.

By contrast, Germany, Austria and Denmark have the least favourable tax and legal environments for private equity industries.

Capital providers' supply of new funds

For capital providers' supply of new funds, it has been argued that the level of capital gains taxes plays a key role; the higher capital gains tax rates are, the lower the incentives for capital providers to invest in private equity. However, some countries that have capital gains tax rates, such as the United States and the United Kingdom, also have high levels of private equity investments (OECD 2002a). Among European countries, the capital gains tax rates differ for corporations and individuals. They also differ according to asset classes and holding periods (OECD 2002b). For example, Belgium does not impose capital gains taxes at the corporate and individual level, while Greece, the Netherlands and Switzerland do not impose capital gains taxes on shares held by individuals (OECD 2002b).

Table 2.4 shows capital gains tax rates for individuals in European countries. In some countries, such as Belgium and Switzerland, capital gains are tax-exempt. In other countries, such as Germany and Denmark, the capital gains tax rates for individuals depend on the individuals' income tax rates. In other countries, such as Portugal, capital gains tax rates depend on the length of time shares are held. Overall, the capital gains tax rates for individuals vary from 0 per cent in Portugal to around 30 per cent in the Scandinavian countries, and even 43 per cent in Denmark.

Providing tax incentives can increase capital providers' incentives to supply funds for private equity investments. These incentives come in two forms: front-end incentives and back-end incentives (OECD 2002b). Under front-end incentives, capital providers receive tax credits for income taxes when investments are qualified (tax reliefs are based on the investment amount). Under back-end incentives, capital providers receive reductions on capital gains taxes for qualifying investments (tax reliefs are based on realized capital gains). Tax incentives can either be related to particular private equity companies, or to particular private equity funds. Tax incentives usually aim at increasing the incentives for capital providers to supply equity capital to particular firms such as young high-technology firms. Several European countries provide tax incentives for investments in private equity funds with an investment focus on the firms' early stage of development.

There are several examples of tax incentives for the private equity companies: the Unternehmensbeteiligungsgesellschaften (under the UBBG) introduced in Germany in the mid-1980s, and the Sociétés

Table 2.4 Important regulations in Europe

This table reports various regulations in European countries. Days and costs are for starting a private limited company. FCPR (Fonds Commun de Placement à Risques) are mutual venture capital funds, AKES are closed-end venture capital mutual funds. BES denotes Business Investment Scheme, EIS denotes Enterprise Investment Scheme, VCT denotes Venture Capital Trust.♣ if shares are held longer than 12 months.♠ depending on the individual income tax rate.

	Capital gains taxes for individuals (%)	Tax incentives (€)	Days for starting a company	Costs for starting a company (€)	Days for bankruptcy
Austria	25	25,000	10–20	2,450–3,500	756
Belgium	Tax exempted	YES	32	980	94.5
Denmark	Up to 43♠	–	3–7	6,715	504
Finland	29	–	12–17	285	630
France	26	FCPR	6–10	450	882
Germany	Up to 23.7♠	–	30–40	1,000	1,008
Greece	5	AKES	5	1,500	1,008
Ireland	20	BES	7.5	1,500	70
Italy	12.5	–	30	2,750	1,764
Netherlands	25	50,185	15	1,750	378
Norway	28	–	5–10	1,191–1,787	252
Portugal	0♣	YES	63	650	504
Spain	15	–	30	600	756
Sweden	30	–	5–20	1,657–2,210	378
Switzerland	Tax exempted	YES	12.5	1,365	189
United Kingdom	10	EIS/VCT	5–7	28–114	252

Source: EVCA (2004b).

de Capital Risques introduced in France in 1988 all aim at offering tax incentives to the private equity companies. For example, under certain conditions, Sociétés de Capital Risques are exempted from corporate income tax on income and capital gains realized from investments. In order to qualify for the Sociétés de Capital Risques status, 50 per cent of the Sociétés de Capital Risques' net assets must be invested in unquoted firms (Berwin & Co 1997). Capital providers do not pay capital gains taxes on their Sociétés de Capital Risques' shares if they have held the shares longer than five years (OECD 2002b).

With respect to tax incentives on the level of private equity funds, the French government has created the Fonds Communs de Placement à Risques (FCPRs), and the Fonds Communs de Placement dans l'Innovation (FCPIs). FCPRs (mutual private equity funds), which have been created since 1985, have to invest at least 40 per cent of their investment volume in unquoted firms. The income from the investments in FCPRs is tax-exempt if it is reinvested. This regulation likely results in relatively high amounts of reinvested capital gains in France. FCPIs, which have been created since 1996, are supposed to push up investments in the high-technology firms. FCPIs have to invest at least 60 per cent of their assets in innovative unquoted firms (Berwin & Co 1997). While FCPIs offer front-end incentives, FCPRs offer back-end incentives for investors. The British goverment has created the Venture Capital Trust (VCT) Scheme in 1995. VCT companies are listed on the London Stock Exchange and are often managed by fund managers of larger investment groups. The VCT scheme offers front-end and back-end incentives for investors.

The capital providers' supply of new funds for private equity investments is also affected by the design of the legal system; by such things as anti-director rights and accounting standards. Table 2.5 provides information on anti-director rights and accounting standards in European countries. Anti-director rights is an index of minority shareholder rights. Higher values mean higher shareholder protection, implying that minority investors have higher incentives for providing equity finance than credit finance. Accounting standards inform how many of the 90 accounting items were included in the 1990 annual reports of firms. Higher values mean better accounting standards, implying lower costs in information gathering for outside investors. These indexes are based on information for large firms only. Therefore, they can give only an indication of accounting standards for private-equity-backed firms.

With respect to anti-director rights, Belgium, Germany, and Italy provide low protection for minority shareholders, while Ireland, Norway, Spain and the United Kingdom provide comparatively high protection for minority shareholders. With respect to accounting standards, firms operating in Sweden include as many as 83 accounting items, while firms operating in Portugal include few accounting items.

Table 2.5 Legal environment in Europe
This table reports legal environment indexes for European countries. Anti-director rights is an index of minority shareholder rights. The index ranges from 0 to 5. Higher values mean higher minority shareholder protection. Accounting standards is an index of how many of the 90 accounting items were included in the 1990 annual reports of firms. Higher values mean higher accounting standards.

	Anti-director rights	Accounting standards
Austria	2	54
Belgium	0	61
Denmark	2	62
Finland	3	77
France	3	69
Germany	1	62
Greece	2	55
Ireland	4	na
Italy	1	62
Netherlands	2	64
Norway	4	74
Portugal	3	36
Spain	4	64
Sweden	3	83
Switzerland	2	68
United Kingdom	5	78

Source: La Porta *et al.* (2000).

Thus, information gathering for outside investors is likely to be easier and less costly in Sweden than in Portugal.

Portfolio firms' demand

The portfolio firms' demand for private equity may be determined by capital gains taxes and corporate taxes, administrative conditions for setting up firms, the research environment, and also bankruptcy and insolvency regulations. Capital gains taxes and corporate taxes determine the incentives for entrepreneurship. Poterba (1989) has argued that the private equity demand is more elastic when capital gains are treated in a favourable way, since this encourages entrepreneurship. According to a composite indicator of tax features related to small firms, Ireland has the most favourable tax regime for entrepreneurs, followed by Italy and the United Kingdom (OECD 2002b). In addition, several countries, such as Belgium, France, Greece, Ireland, the Netherlands, Portugal, Spain and the United Kingdom have lower corporate tax rates for small firms (OECD 2002b).

The administrative conditions for setting up firms vary substantially in European countries (Table 2.4). The number of days necessary for starting up private limited companies ranges from three to seven days in Denmark to 30 to 40 days in Germany. Administrative costs for starting private limited companies range from €28 to €114 in the United Kingdom to €6,715 in Denmark. Combining the information on days and costs for starting private limited companies indicates that entrepreneurial conditions in the United Kingdom and France are comparatively good, while in Germany and Italy they are comparatively bad.

While taxes and administrative conditions are likewise important for all start-up firms in an economy, the research environment is likely to be more important for starting up a high-technology firm than for starting up a firm operating in a traditional industry. Incentives for firms to engage in research and development activities can be fiscal incentives, and incentives that work through patent regulations. Ueda (2004) has shown in his theoretical model that a legal environment favouring strong protection of intellectual property rights encourages private equity demand. Patents are important for protecting ideas for a short period in order to obtain monopoly rents important for compensating high research and development efforts.

Bankruptcy and insolvency regulations may affect developments in private equity industries as well. In the United States, going bankrupt (declaring 'chapter eleven') is considered a risk of doing business, while in Europe it is still seen as a major setback to the social status of any business (Dehesa 2002). More specifically, an important factor for the private equity demand is whether financial intermediaries, employees, and also family and friends see the bankruptcy of a high-technology firm as a failure or whether they acknowledge the business spirit of the founder and give him/her another chance with a new business idea. Important in this respect is also the time required between the declaration of bankruptcy and the closure of proceedings because it may determine the point in time when the entrepreneur who failed with his/her business idea comes up with a new business idea. The average time in bankruptcy varies across European countries, as Table 2.4 indicates. In Ireland and Belgium less than 100 days are required, while in Germany, Greece and Italy more than 1,000 days are required.

Private equity companies

The tax and legal environments affect the investment behaviour of private equity companies as well. A key element in this respect is the handling of management fees and carried interests, which compensate the managers of private equity funds for their efforts in selecting and supporting high-technology firms financed with the funds' capital, that are liable to value-added tax (VAT) in some countries. In Austria, management fees and carried interests are liable to VAT. In Finland, Ireland, the Netherlands, Spain and Sweden, management fees and carried interests are not necessarily liable to VAT, while in Belgium, Greece, Italy, Norway and the United Kingdom they are not liable to VAT. Management fees are liable to VAT in Germany, while they are not in Portugal. Carried interests are liable to VAT in Portugal, while they are not in France and Germany.

The investment behaviour of private equity companies is also affected by government subsidies. European governments try to boost private equity investments in high-technology start-ups by utilizing various subsidy schemes such as guarantee and co-investment schemes. Under a guarantee scheme, the government covers a share of private equity companies' realized losses. Under a co-investment scheme, a government-based private equity company invests funds that supplement those from non-government-based private equity companies in start-up firms. In the United Kingdom, the government has created several funds, such as the enterprise fund and the early growth fund, to increase equity access for small firms (Baygan 2003a). In France, the Société Francaise de Garantie des Financements des Petites et Moyennes Entreprises (SOFARIS) is the main loan guarantor agency owned by the government, financial institutions and insurance companies (OECD 1997). SOFARIS guarantees private equity companies' investments in start-up firms up to 65 per cent of the investment volume (Lessat *et al.* 1999). In Germany, the Kreditanstalt für Wiederaufbau (KfW) is the main loan guarantor agency owned by the government. Under the loan scheme of the Beteiligungsprogramm für kleine Technologieunternehmen (BTU) introduced in 1995, the KfW refinances 70 per cent of private equity investors' participations in small and often young high-technology firms, up to a maximum amount of €2 million. Under the co-investment scheme, the KfW invests as a non-active co-investor, up to a maximum amount of €1.5 million, if a non-government-based private equity company, the so-called lead investor, invests at least the same amount in the form of equity and if the lead investor supports the management team and monitors the development of the firm. In Spain, the Nuevas Empresas Tecnológicas initiative provides soft loans to start-up firms (Tejada 2003a).

The complexity and variety of the tax and legal environments concerning capital providers' supply of new funds, portfolio firms' demand for private equity and the investment behaviour of private equity companies in Europe make the identification of those factors that may mainly hinder the development of private equity industries a difficult task. The Organization for Economic Co-operation and Development (OECD) has identified those factors that may limit the private equity demand by start-up firms (OECD 2002b). Moreover, the EVCA has undertaken several studies in order to identify those factors hindering the development of liquid private equity industries in Europe. However, it is not clear, whether factors related to the supply side are more hindering than factors related to the demand side of private equity finance.

Summary

This chapter has given an overview of the sizes of private equity industries around the globe. Compared to the United States, private equity industries in Europe are comparatively small. However, some European countries have been relatively successful in catching up. One explanation for the differences in the sizes of private equity industries discussed in this chapter is the tax and legal environments affecting either the capital providers' supply of new funds for private equity investments, the portfolio firms' demand for private equity, or the investment behaviour of private equity companies themselves.

3
Fundraising

This chapter deals with private equity companies and their fundraising behaviour. Fundraising is the first of three phases in the venture capital cycle. In the fundraising phase, private equity companies build up their relationship with capital providers from which private equity companies raise their funds for private equity investments. The two other phases, the investing and exiting phase, are at the centre of Chapter 4 and Chapter 5.

The first part of this chapter describes various sources of heterogeneity among private equity companies, such as the type of capital providers from which private equity companies raise new funds. This heterogeneity is important to understand investment patterns in European private equity industries. The second part offers information on the relationship between private equity companies and their capital providers.

Heterogeneity of private equity companies

The heterogeneity of private equity companies has at least four sources. Private equity companies are heterogeneous regarding their relationship to governments, their investment focus, their capital providers and their reputation and experience. These four sources of heterogeneity are discussed in the following.

Government-based companies

The first source of heterogeneity is related to the role of governments in financing high-technology firms. In European markets, both non-government-based and government-based private equity companies are active. Government-based companies invest often jointly with non-government-based companies in high-technology firms. They differ in their aims to offer capital to high-technology firms. Non-government-based private equity companies aim at realizing maximum returns for a given level of risk. In contrast, government-based companies are most often non-profit oriented.

Generally, funding from the government for financing small firms either by establishing government-based private equity companies, or by offering capital in another direct or indirect way (for example, *via* a non-government-based company) is justified by using the following rationales. First, it is argued that small firms, especially those operating in high-technology industries, can generate positive externalities and spillovers (Gebhardt and Schmidt 2002, Lerner 2002a). In the case of spillovers, innovators receive only a part of the social returns on their innovations (Griliches 1992, Jaffe 1996). In this case, the social returns from realizing a business idea exceed the private returns that the innovators can appropriate. This difference between social and private returns leads to underinvestment in business ideas. Second, it is argued that asymmetric information between investors in and founders of firms results in a market failure, implying capital shortages especially for those firms that are young and that operate in high-technology industries. Young firms have no track record. Therefore, market failures in the form of capital shortages are likely to be more severe for younger than for older firms (see, *inter alia*, Bond *et al.* 1999, Egeln *et al.* 1997, Harhoff 1998, Himmelberg and Petersen 1994, Barlow and Robson 2002). Firms operating in high-technology industries may even be more severely capital-constrained because high-technology industries are more likely to be characterized by a high degree of asset intangibility and a high degree of investment risks than traditional industries. A high degree of asset intangibility implies the non-availability of particular financial control mechanisms such as collateral.

These rationales are, however, not sufficient for establishing government funding schemes for small firms, or young high-technology firms (see, for example, Hyytinen and Väänänen 2003). Generally, government funding is not likely to solve or mitigate adverse selection problems between financial intermediaries and young high-technology firms. Thus, government funding cannot help in selecting single firms out of a large number of young high-technology firms seeking finance. It can only offer funding to all young high-technology firms in a similar way. At the same time, government funding may even decrease efficiency in financial markets, as recent theoretical literature has argued. For credit markets, De Meza (2002) has shown that efficiency decreases because problems of adverse selection are increased. Murray and Marriot (1998) have argued that government funding reduces venture capital companies' incentives to carefully select the most promising firms for investments. If the firms differ regarding their quality, the fact that the government covers a substantial amount of the costs in case of a failure leads to lower costs of adverse selection for venture capital companies. Thus, under public subsidies, venture capital companies have to bear lower costs if they select a 'lemon'. In addition, Schertler (2003) has shown that an investment subsidy attracts more inexperienced venture capital companies to the market, resulting, under certain conditions, in inefficient capital allocation. Moreover, Keuschnigg and Nielsen (2001) have argued that venture capital companies have incentives to finance more firms when the government offers subsidies. Apart from these arguments against governments' subsidies, these subsidies also in the form of investments provided by government-based venture capital companies can crowd out private investments (European Commission 2000).

To give an impression of the relative importance of government-based private equity companies, I use information from the VCPro dataset described in detail in Table A1. Table A2 offers the definition of the variables used in the following. Table 3.1 provides an overview of the total number of private equity companies in European countries in the VCPro dataset, of the total number of members in national venture capital associations and of the importance of government-based companies. A comparison of the number of companies in the VCPro database and the number of venture capital and private equity companies that are members of national venture capital associations indicates that the VCPro database includes many private equity companies active in European countries. According to Table 3.1, the United Kingdom has the highest number of private equity companies, followed by Germany. Portugal and Greece have a very low number of private equity companies. Belgium and Portugal have a relatively high percentage of government-based private equity companies.

For some countries, the information offered in Table 3.1 understates the relevance of government-based private equity companies. More specifically, Bascha and Walz (2002b) have analysed the fundraising behaviour of German private equity companies. They conducted a survey of all the regular members of the German venture capital association. In their sample, all private equity companies are classified as non-government-based if their ownership structure indicates that it is not subject to either direct or indirect government

Table 3.1 Number of private equity companies
This table reports the number of private equity companies in European countries. The number VCNA reports the number of members of the national venture capital organizations and is taken from Bottazzi *et al.* (2004a). Generalists are those companies either classified as private equity company or as public venture capital company in the VCPro dataset. Specialists are those companies classified as venture capital company. Government is those companies classified as government-based companies.

	Number		Percentage of number in VCPro dataset		
	VCPro	VCNA	Generalists	Specialists	Government
Austria	25	23	60.00	40.00	0.00
Belgium	34	34	26.47	61.76	11.76
Denmark	26	29	38.46	53.85	7.69
Finland	34	33	29.41	61.76	8.82
France	64	101	50.00	48.44	1.56
Germany	119	146	31.09	68.91	0.00
Greece	11	8	27.27	72.73	0.00
Ireland	18	15	16.67	83.33	0.00
Italy	22	37	63.64	36.36	0.00
Netherlands	33	52	27.27	69.70	3.03
Norway	19	22	26.32	73.68	0.00
Portugal	9	10	66.67	22.22	11.11
Spain	24	38	70.83	25.00	4.17
Sweden	84	17	28.57	69.05	2.38
Switzerland	44	43	38.64	61.36	0.00
United Kingdom	202	139	44.06	54.95	0.99
Total	768	747	39.06	58.72	2.21

Source: VCPro Dataset, Bottazzi *et al.* (2004a), own calculations.

influence. According to their definition, 43 per cent of the German private equity companies are government-based companies.

Investment focus

The second source of heterogeneity is related to the investment focus of private equity companies. Some private equity companies are not specialized regarding firms' development stages. Other private equity companies are specialized in either financing management buy-out deals or financing the firms in their early stage of development. For example, *BPE Private Equity GmbH*, which was founded in 1998, is specialized in financing management buy-out deals. *BASF Venture Capital GmbH*, which was founded in 2001, is specialized in financing firms in their early stage of development.

The VCPro database allows distinguishing between *generalists*, which are private equity companies that have either a broad investment strategy or which are specialized in management buy-out investments, and *specialists*, which are private equity companies that invest in the early stage and expansion stage of firms' development. Thus, specialists may be interpreted as venture capital companies in the US–American tradition. However, specialists in this sample do not necessarily provide management support services, as US–American venture capital companies do. Table 3.1 offers information on the relevance of these two types of private equity companies. In the minority of countries, Austria, Italy, Portugal and Spain, the number of generalists is higher than the number of specialists. In other countries, such as Ireland and Norway, more than 70 per cent are specialists.

The VCPro dataset allows funds under management of the private equity companies to be looked at. On average, each company manages €580 million. The amount of funds under management varies among the various types of companies; generalists manage on average more than €980 million, while specialists manage on average only €320 million, and government-based companies manage almost €330 million. Using this dataset, I estimated whether the volume of funds under management

Table 3.2 Funds size
This table reports estimation results for private equity companies' volume of funds under management. The volume of funds under management is the endogenous variable (in millions of euros). The estimation method used is OLS. Country dummies are included in all estimations. Absolute heteroscedasticity-consistent t-statistics are shown below the coefficients.***, **, denotes significance at 1, 5 and 10 per cent levels.

	(1)	(2)
Specialists	–635.983***	–576.165***
	(3.67)	(3.11)
Government-based company	–481.095**	–657.566**
	(2.02)	(2.47)
Founding year		–33.702**
		(2.32)
Constant	530.260***	67,393.721**
	(3.6)	(2.33)
Number of observations	632	582
F-test	3.332	3.19
Adjusted R^2	0.053	0.11

Source: VCPro dataset, own calculations.

varies significantly with the types of the company. Table 3.2 reports estimation results using a linear regression model. The regression results indicate that specialists and government-based companies manage significantly less funds than generalists.

Apart from the type of the company and the volume of funds under management, the VCPro dataset allows the age of private equity companies to be looked at. Therefore, I checked whether the age of the private equity companies affects the amount of funds under management. The results, which are presented in Table 3.2, show the volume of funds under management increases with the age of the private equity company. The more recent the founding year of a company is, that is, the younger the company is, the smaller the volume of funds under management. This result holds also when the sample is restricted to either only generalists or only specialists. Older private equity companies manage most often more than one fund implying a higher volume of funds under management, while very young private equity companies may have just raised their first fund.

Capital providers

The third source of heterogeneity is related to the fundraising of private equity companies. Non-government-based private equity companies can be distinguished in dependent and independent private equity companies. Private equity companies are dependent on their capital providers when they are a subsidiary of their capital providers. Private and savings banks, and corporations are more likely to set up subsidiaries because then they can determine investment decisions directly. Private equity companies are independent of their capital providers when they raise funds in financial markets. Pension funds and insurance companies are more likely to invest in independent private equity companies.

Capital providers are likely to differ in their aims to offer capital for venture capital and management buy-out investments, and thus in the kind of capital they provide. Private banks may be interested in investing equity capital in those firms in which they also hold debt claims. Hellmann *et al.* (2004) have argued that banks want to build up relationships with firms early in order to use these contacts later on for their lending business. Because of banks' risk aversion and investment strategy one may argue that funds provided by banks are more likely to be invested in less risky investment projects. Bank-dependent private equity companies have the expertise to structure the deals. However, compared to US venture capital companies they lack the expertise to add value to their portfolio firms and to access trends and technologies (Hardymon *et al.* 2003). Engel (2003b) has argued that bank-dependent private equity companies are more likely to demand lower rates of returns than independent private equity companies. Private equity companies owned by savings banks may promote only firms in the region in which they operate (Kulicke 2001).

Non-financial corporations may have an interest in building cooperative relationships and in keeping an eye on new technological developments (Riyanto and Schwienbacher 2002, Schween 1996, Birkinshaw *et al.* 2002). In contrast to dependent private equity companies, independent private equity companies may not have other aims than realizing high returns for a given level of risk.

To give an impression of the relevance of various types of capital providers, Table 3.3 reports new funds provided by various capital providers as a percentage of total new funds raised averaged over the years 1991 to 2003. This table is based on the EVCA statistics, which allow distinguishing between eight capital providers for new funds; corporations, private individuals, governments, banks, pension funds, insurance companies, academic institutions, and realized capital gains. Banks were the most relevant source of new funds with about 32 per cent over all countries and years. Realized capital gains accounted for about 18 per cent of new funds raised. Pension funds contributed only 11 per cent followed by corporations, governments and insurance companies, which contributed about 9 per cent of the new funds raised for private equity investments. Private individuals accounted for 7 per cent, while academic institutions, which accounted for about 1 per cent, played an insignificant role.

During the observation period, the relevance of capital providers as a source of new funds differed substantially across European countries. Corporations played a more important role in Finland and Norway, while they played a minor role in the Netherlands, Austria and Denmark. Private individuals contributed substantial amounts in Norway and Ireland, while they were non-existent in Portugal. Governments played an important role as a source of new funds in Portugal, while they contributed little in Switzerland. Banks were dominant in all countries of continental Europe except the Scandinavian countries. Pension funds were important in the United Kingdom and in Sweden, while they played little role in Greece and Portugal. Insurance companies were relevant in Finland and France, while they were irrelevant in Belgium, Denmark, Ireland and Portugal. Realized capital gains were a very important source of funds in several countries, such as in Belgium, Denmark and Norway.

Table 3.3 Capital providers

This table reports new funds raised from various capital providers as a percentage of new funds raised, averaged over the years 1991 to 2003. Time trend is the coefficient of a time trend in a fixed effects model including year dummies, where the endogenous variable is the share of new funds provided by the various capital providers. **(*) denotes significance at the 5 (10) per cent level.

	Corporations	Private individuals	Governments	Banks	Pension funds	Insurance companies	Academic institutions	Realized capital gains
Austria	5.4	6.4	15.7	54.3	2.8	5.5	0.0	3.0
Belgium	9.0	6.8	7.1	25.6	3.0	2.4	0.6	39.6
Denmark	5.5	7.5	6.2	21.9	18.9	2.6	0.1	32.2
Finland	16.5	1.3	14.2	16.0	16.7	18.9	0.2	2.9
France	8.9	11.5	6.2	51.5	11.5	19.8	11.4	25.4
Germany	8.2	6.6	9.9	46.4	6.0	13.2	0.1	1.8
Greece	10.8	6.9	6.8	39.1	1.2	3.7	0.0	20.1
Ireland	3.7	13.7	10.2	23.2	13.8	2.5	0.4	17.3
Italy	8.5	10.3	2.5	51.8	3.2	4.3	0.0	11.9
Netherlands	4.4	2.8	2.0	35.3	9.6	13.1	0.2	24.9
Norway	16.1	14.6	6.2	5.7	2.1	9.8	0.2	36.8
Portugal	5.8	0.2	24.7	43.7	0.0	2.3	0.0	16.4
Spain	10.6	5.4	14.7	37.6	9.4	3.9	0.0	4.6
Sweden	11.4	3.2	9.4	8.0	26.3	12.8	1.7	9.5
Switzerland	8.9	10.7	0.7	38.3	10.5	4.6	2.0	15.3
United Kingdom	6.6	3.8	3.3	17.3	34.4	13.5	1.4	9.7
Total	8.8	7.0	8.7	31.7	11.0	8.5	1.2	17.7
Time trend	–0.13	–0.15	0.83**	–1.25*	0.46	0.24	0.03	0.87*

Source: EVCA (various issues), own calculations.

One reason for the differences in the relative importance of pension funds and insurance companies as capital providers of new funds for private equity investments is that the assets managed by these financial companies differ substantially in size across European countries. In 2001, financial assets of pension funds accounted for 114 per cent of GDP in Switzerland and 66 per cent in the United Kingdom, while they accounted for less than 5 per cent in Austria, Finland, France, Germany, Italy and Sweden (OECD 2003a). Financial assets of insurance companies accounted for more than 60 per cent of GDP in France, Sweden, Switzerland and the United Kingdom, while they accounted for less than 30 per cent in Spain and Portugal (OECD 2003a).

Thus, assets under management of pension funds and insurance companies may help in explaining the relative importance of pension funds as capital providers in the United Kingdom, and the relative importance of insurance companies in France. However, assets under management fail to explain the relative unimportance of pension funds in providing new funds for private equity in Switzerland, and the importance of pension funds in providing new funds in Sweden.

A second and even more important reason for the different relevance of pension funds and insurance companies is that investment regulations determine the percentage of the pension funds' or insurance companies' assets invested in high-risk assets such as private equity. Only three European countries, Ireland, the Netherlands and the United Kingdom, have a prudent man rule (EVCA 2004a). In other European countries, pension funds can often invest in this asset class but with a quantitative limitation. In Belgium pension funds and insurance companies can invest up to 10 per cent of their assets in shares not traded in an organized capital market (EVCA 2004a). In Germany, pension funds have no quantitative limitations, but the supervisory authority has to approve the investment allocation (EVCA 2004a). In Spain, pension funds and insurance companies can invest up to 10 per cent of their assets in unlisted firms (Tejada 2003a). In Portugal, pension funds can invest 15 per cent of their assets in unquoted firms since December 2002 (Tejada 2003b) (previously they could invest 3 per cent). In Norway, insurance companies may invest not more than 5 per cent of their assets in high-risk assets (Baygan 2003b).

A third reason for the different relevance of pension funds and insurance companies is that these financial companies invest internationally. Some countries had new funds provided by pension funds even if pension funds in these countries did not have significant assets under management. For example, in Germany pension funds provided some funds for private equity investment in the mid of the 1990s. These new funds were not provided by German pension funds but by British and Dutch pension funds.

In order to gain insights into the developments of the relative importance of capital providers as sources of new funds over time, I ran one simple fixed-effects regression for each capital provider *f* of the following empirical model:

$$S_{ift} = C_{if} + \beta_f \, trend_{ft} + e_{ift} \tag{3.1}$$

where S_{ift} denotes the new funds raised from a particular capital provider *f* as a percentage of total new funds raised in country *i* in year *t*, $trend_{ft}$ is a time trend, which informs on the relative importance of capital providers over time, and ε_{ift} is the error term. Equation (3.1) was estimated using a fixed effects estimator that removes country-specific time-invariant intercepts, C_{if}, by calculating the means of all variables under consideration (Wooldridge 2002).

According to the coefficients of the time trend reported in Table 3.3, the importance of governments as a source of new funds for private equity investments increased in the period under consideration. In addition, the relative importance of capital gains as source of new funds increased. In contrast, the relative importance of banks declined significantly over time.

In addition to the capital providers, the EVCA statistics distinguish between independent, dependent, semi-dependent and government-based private equity companies. Table 3.4 reports investments by these particular types of private equity companies as a percentage of total private equity investments averaged over the years 1991 to 2003. According to this table, independent private equity companies accounted for 54 per cent of the total private equity investments. Dependent private equity companies accounted for 20 per cent, followed by semi-dependent and government-based companies, which accounted for 15 and 11 per cent, respectively. The coefficients of a time trend of a fixed-effects regression model indicate that the share of investments provided by government-based companies declined significantly in recent years. Thus, while the relative importance of governments as a source of new funds increased over time, the relative importance regarding investments declined. This might indicate that governments provided new funds more often to non-government-based companies than to government-based companies. The time trend for the shares of all other types of private equity companies is, however, insignificant.

The relevance of independent and dependent private equity companies varied between European countries. Relative to the countries' private equity industries, independent private equity companies were important in Austria, Denmark and Sweden, to name just a few. Dependent private equity companies played an important role as capital providers in Greece and Italy, while semi-dependent providers played an important role in Portugal. Government-based companies played an important role in Belgium and Finland.

Not only did the importance of the various types of private equity companies vary across European countries, it also varied over time. In France, for example, the share of investments by independent private equity companies was as low as 33 per cent in 1994. However, the

Table 3.4 Types of private equity companies
This table reports investments by particular types of private equity companies as a percentage of private equity investments, averaged over the years 1991 to 2003. Time trend is the coefficient of a time trend in a fixed effects model including year dummies, where the endogenous variable is the share of investments by various types of private equity companies. ** denotes significance at the 5 per cent level.

	Independent	Dependent	Semi-dependent	Government-based
Austria	72.0	11.7	12.3	4.0
Belgium	23.2	21.8	8.9	46.2
Denmark	84.0	7.5	6.3	2.3
Finland	42.7	10.7	9.5	36.6
France	44.3	27.7	27.1	1.0
Germany	53.1	26.6	6.9	9.1
Greece	43.9	41.3	8.7	0.0
Ireland	54.1	15.0	25.1	5.8
Italy	38.2	39.3	11.9	10.5
Netherlands	52.4	36.8	6.3	5.6
Norway	63.5	6.7	5.9	23.9
Portugal	23.6	25.8	36.2	14.4
Spain	63.9	10.6	20.3	5.1
Sweden	70.2	12.3	11.3	6.2
Switzerland	60.4	28.3	11.2	0.0
United Kingdom	64.9	15.7	18.9	0.4
Total	53.8	20.5	14.7	10.8
Time trend	0.80	–0.06	0.38	–1.06**

Source: EVCA (various issues), own calculations.

share increased substantially in recent years and reached almost 78 per cent in 2003. A similar movement took place in Germany: the share of new funds raised by independent private equity companies increased significantly.

However, in other countries such as Austria, Belgium, Italy and the United Kingdom the share of new funds raised by independent private equity companies did not change significantly over time. In contrast, in a third group of countries, such as Denmark, the share of new funds raised by independent private equity companies decreased significantly over time.

Funds are not always provided by capital providers directly but by funds-of-funds investment vehicles, whose activity increased substantially at the end of the 1990s. The EVCA reports 74 companies managing funds-of-funds activity in Europe. 34 per cent are located in the United Kingdom, 17 per cent in Germany and Switzerland. The average fund volume increased from €164 million in 1990-1993 to more than €390 million in 1999. After the bursting of the stock market bubble in 2000 average fund volume stayed on relatively high levels. In 2001 (2002), the average fund volume was €305 (281) million. This indicates that some private equity companies were able to raise substantial amounts of funds even conditions for raising funds deteriorated significantly (VentureCapital Magazin 9/2003: p. 29).

The group of dependent private equity companies is a very broad class, since it contains private equity companies that are dependent on private banks, savings banks and non-financial corporations. These capital providers are likely to differ in their incentives to provide capital for venture capital and management buy-out investments. To a certain extent, all capital providers aim at receiving an appropriate rate of return on their funds. However, they may differ with respect to additional goals, as I have argued above. These aims of the capital providers are transmitted to the private equity companies, with important implications for the reputation building and experience accumulation of private equity companies. In particular, bank-dependent private equity companies are unlikely to accumulate industry-specific technological experience, since they finance firms in a multitude of different industries in later stages of firms' development. Therefore, they are unlikely to certify the quality of high-technology firms when the firms are going to public equity markets. However, bank-dependent private equity companies may be advantageous for high-technology firms when going public for other reasons, such as their network contacts to other banks, and underwriters.

Information on the various types of dependent private equity companies comes from the German and the French VC datasets. Details on these datasets are provided in Table A1 and Table A2. The German VC dataset of private equity companies contains information on 143 private equity companies; 66 are independent private equity companies, 31 are dependent on private banks, 26 are dependent on savings banks, 18 are dependent on the government and two are dependent on non-financial corporations. The largest sub-group of the government-based companies is the Mittelständische Beteiligungsgesellschaften (MBGs),[3] which often offer only silent partnerships and which have a strict geographical investment focus. The French VC dataset contains information on 128 private equity companies; 59 are independent private equity companies, 55 are dependent on banks, nine are dependent on non-financial corporations, and five are dependent on insurance companies.

In the German VC dataset, corporate private equity companies are underrepresented. At the end of the 1990s, several of Germany's large corporations founded corporate private equity companies that invest in high-technology firms, which are, however, not included in the dataset. For example, in 1999, Siemens founded the *Siemens Venture Capital GmbH,* which nowadays has €60 million funds under management.[4] BASF founded the *BASF Venture Capital GmbH* in 2001 with €100 million of funds under management.[5]

For Germany, Tykvova (2004) has reported that bank-dependent and government-based private equity companies are typically bridge investors, while independent and corporate private equity companies are more similar to US venture capital companies. Bascha and Walz (2002b) have found that especially young private equity companies are most similar to US venture capital companies.

Reputation and experience

The fourth source of heterogeneity is related to the reputation of venture capital companies in raising new funds, and their experience in financing high-technology firms. Venture capital companies' reputation and experience is important at different points of time during the venture capital cycle. Reputation in raising new funds may be important when determining contract conditions between venture capital companies and capital providers. Moreover, reputation may be important to certify the quality of portfolio firms to other market participants when a portfolio firm goes public or is sold. Experience in financing high-technology firms may be important for successfully selecting high-technology firms out of a large number of firms seeking finance. Moreover, experience may determine the quality of monitoring and management support services provided by venture capital companies to the portfolio firms.

Empirically, these different sources of heterogeneity are often difficult to identify precisely. However, for analysing whether private equity and venture capital companies add value to their portfolio firms (see Chapter 4) or whether they certify the quality of their portfolio firms to other less-informed investors (see Chapter 5) it is necessary to take these sources of heterogeneity into account.

The relationship to capital providers

The relationship between private equity companies and their capital providers has many interesting facets but few studies have empirically analysed this relationship for Europe, mainly because datasets for econometric analysis are not available. In the following, I discuss two facets that have been addressed in the recent literature: the design of contracts between independent private equity companies and capital providers, and capital transfer between private equity companies and capital providers.

Design of contracts

Regarding the design of the contracts between private equity companies and capital providers, Feinendegen *et al.* (2002) have offered a descriptive study for European countries. They have described the existence of incentive compensation systems and covenants using information on 122 fund prospectuses and 46 partnership agreements between 1996 and 2001. They have restricted their analysis to limited partnerships only (another legal form is the publicly listed company). According to their study, most private equity funds are legally constituted as a limited partnership with a pre-determined, finite lifetime (closed-end form).[6]

Limited partnerships are very popular as an organizational form for venture capital and private equity companies in the United Kingdom and the United States (Lerner 1995, Barnes and McCarthy 2002). In a limited partnership, the general partners (the venture capital companies) are independent of their limited partners (their capital providers). In the United States, institutional investors find limited partnerships attractive, since taxes are paid only by the (taxable) investors but not by the limited partnership (Gompers and Lerner 1998). Limited partnerships have to fulfill several legal constraints. They must have a pre-determined, finite lifetime (usually ten years). Participation of limited partners in the active management is forbidden, and the transfer of limited partnerships' shares is restricted (Sahlman 1990). The limited and pre-specified lifetime of the funds might be advantageous, since it can protect the limited partners against the possibility that the general partner could act against the interests of limited partners (Sahlman 1990). In addition, as Brouwer and Hendrix (1998) have argued, the limited and pre-specified lifetime of funds seems to make it easier for venture capital companies to invest in start-up firms and to exit from their participation in portfolio firms in time.

In Germany, the predominant organizational form of private equity funds changed from unlimited open funds (so-called evergreens) to limited closed funds at the end of 1990s. At the beginning of the 1990s, private equity funds were often organized as funds without specified time frames or volumes, while at the end of the 1990s, more than 60 per cent of the new funds were raised by closed funds (BVK 2000). This was not caused by a change in the behaviour of the private equity companies already acting in the industry at the beginning of the 1990s, but by a large number of young and independent private equity companies that entered the industry at the end of the 1990s and refinanced themselves with closed funds (Bascha and Walz 2002b).

However, the limited and pre-specified lifetime of the funds may also give private equity companies incentives to abandon investments prematurely and to select only firms from which they can exit in time. Furthermore, it must be kept in mind that private equity companies, when they are independent from their capital providers, are not only interested in the performance of the firms in their portfolios but also in raising new funds. Gifford (1997) has shown in a theoretical model that private equity companies spend less time on management support in the firm than would be optimal from the portfolio firms' point of view, as well as from the capital providers' point of view, since private equity companies need time to raise new funds and to provide management support services to portfolio firms. In contrast, dependent private equity companies can concentrate exclusively on supporting the management of the firms in their portfolios. However, they may lack the experience to do so.

Recently, an alternative model for raising funds was developed (Smith 2004b). In April 2004, *Apollo* introduced a publicly traded investment vehicle and raised $930 million in an initial public offering. Quoted vehicles offer the possibility to capital providers to move in and out daily. Private equity companies managing quoted vehicles also adopt management fees and carried interests, which are described for traditional limited partnerships below.

The contract between the private equity company and the capital providers aims at solving several incentive problems that may arise because information is asymmetrically distributed between the private equity company and capital providers. An incentive compensation contains, in addition to a fixed payment, a flexible payment that is tied to the performance of the funds.[7] Because of this performance-dependent compensation, relatively low-qualified managers would not start a private equity company. Moreover, because of this performance-dependent compensation, general partners of private equity companies have stronger incentives to improve the selection of firms and management support services they provide to the firms in their portfolios.

In partnership agreements and similarly for publicly traded investment vehicles, the management fee and carried interests are specified for the whole lifetime of the funds. The management fee is independent from the performance of the funds, while the carried interests depend on the performance of the funds. Regarding management fees, general partners receive an annual management fee of usually around 2.5 per cent of the capital committed (Sahlman 1990). Feinendegen *et al.* (2002) have reported that the nominal management fee rates are very similar in their European sample. However, they have found substantial differences when calculating the present value of management fees that has to be paid over the whole lifetime of the funds. Specifically, they have reported management fees ranging from 2.5 per cent of the committed capital to 24.2 per cent, the average being 14.7 per cent. Regarding carried interest, 90 per cent of the general partners of European private equity funds analysed by Feinendegen *et al.* (2002) received 20 per cent of the realized gains of the funds. In the United States, about 80 per cent of the general partners receive 20 per cent of the realized gains, 15 per cent receive 25 per cent of the realized gains, and 5 per cent receive even 30 per cent of the realized gains.

This compensation system can be interpreted as a mechanism that capital providers utilize to offer general partners stronger incentives to carefully monitor and support the portfolio firms after the contract between the general partners and the limited partners has been signed. This is necessary because capital providers cannot monitor whether the general partners fulfill their management support and monitoring function in the portfolio firms or whether they waste their time.

However, this compensation system may induce the general partners to select and to invest in riskier projects, since the general partners participate in increasing profits but not simultaneously in increasing risks. Such behaviour can be limited by using an additional mechanism: the general partners' incentives to select riskier investment projects are reduced when they invest alongside with limited partners in the fund. General partners of already established private equity companies are more often obliged to invest their money in the funds they raise than their counterparts of recently established private equity companies (Schmidt and Wahrenburg 2003).

If the general partners' incentives to invest in riskier projects are sufficiently reduced by investing alongside in the funds, then the limited partners can increase their expected returns by using hurdle rates. Hurdle rates guarantee a minimum return to limited partners before the general partners participate in the performance of the funds, that is, before carried interests have to be paid. However, this control mechanism is relatively seldom used in Europe: 50 per cent of the funds analysed by Feinendegen *et al.* (2002) have not specified a hurdle rate at all, and only 4 per cent have specified a hurdle rate of 10 per cent per annum.

Moreover, general partners' incentives are improved by using covenants that aim at changing the risk-return profile of the funds. Feinendegen *et al.* (2002) have described 14 covenants which either regulate the overall management of funds, or restrict the activities of the fund managers and the types of investments. In 61 per cent of the cases analysed they have found that there are restrictions on the size of single investments, and in 60 per cent of the cases that there are restrictions regarding increases in debt capital. Both covenants aim at reducing the risks of the funds. Moreover, they have found that there are restrictions on the sale of the general partners' fund shares in 54 per cent of the cases analysed. Most interesting is, however, their result regarding the involvement of the limited partners when the composition of the management team of the private equity company changes. Since the performance of the funds is likely to depend on the experience of the fund managers, Feinendegen *et al.* (2002) expected that limited partners would want to participate in decisions regarding the composition in the team of fund managers. But only in 7 per cent of the cases analysed did limited partners have a contractually specified right to do so. This can be the result of strong performance incentives: if general partners have strong performance incentives, the general partners have no incentives to lower the quality and experience in the team of fund managers.

Schmidt and Wahrenburg (2003) have empirically analysed determinants of covenants used between general partners and limited partners of private equity companies. They have found that funds whose managers have managed at least one fund previously are more severely restricted by contractual covenants than funds whose managers are managing their first fund. Moreover, they have found that the number of restrictive covenants is not decreasing in the supply of private equity. By contrast, Gompers and Lerner (1996) have found evidence for the United States that the number of restrictive covenants can be reduced in the case of high levels of venture capital supply. This indicates that venture capital companies can increase their bargaining position *vis-à-vis* capital providers when the venture capital supply increases. Note, that Gompers and Lerner (1996) took the monetary compensation of general partners into account when they explained the numbers of covenants used, while Schmidt and Wahrenburg (2003) did not.

Capital transfer

Regarding the transfer of capital between either private equity companies or portfolio firms, on the one hand, and capital providers, on the other, Ljungqvist and Richardson (2003) have investigated at which point in time capital is returned to capital providers. They used a dataset of 3,800 portfolio firms in several hundred private equity funds between 1981 and 2001, which informs on the precise date of cash-flows between private equity companies and capital providers. According to their data, on average, almost 13 per cent of the total committed capital was returned to the capital providers by the end of the 3rd year. One hundred per cent of the total committed capital was returned by the end of the 7th year.[8]

Ljungqvist and Richardson (2003) have analysed econometrically the time frame in which private equity companies have chosen to return capital to capital providers either by using data on the fund or the portfolio-firm level. On the fund level, this time depends negatively on the number of firms financed in an industry in which the private equity company is interested in investing in. In addition, the time taken to return capital to capital providers depends on the competition for deal flow. In the empirical analysis by Ljungqvist and Richardson (2003), competition for deal flows is captured by the total capital raised by other funds: the higher the competition for deals flow is, the longer the time to return capital to capital providers.

Using a duration model on the portfolio-firm level, Ljungqvist and Richardson (2003) have analysed the time between an investment in a particular portfolio firm and the returning of capital to capital providers. The average holding period is 14 quarters, which is adjusted for right-censored funds. Increasing competition for deal flows, captured by the funds raised by direct competitors, increases holding periods. In addition, the time between an investment in a particular portfolio firm and the returning of capital depends negatively on the investment size. The time between an investment in a particular portfolio firm and the returning of capital is significantly longer for venture capital funds than for management buy-out funds.

Ljungqvist and Richardson (2003) have reported that the average fund of 73 funds raised between 1981 and 1993 has drawn down almost 95 per cent. Over the life cycle of a fund, the drawn downs in the first three years of the fund are almost of equal size, after three years, draw down rates slow down substantially. According to a study by the EVCA (2004a), 63 per cent of the capital committed is drawn down in the first three years of a fund's lifetime.

Using a duration model on the fund level, Ljungqvist and Richardson (2003) have analysed factors that affect the time needed for private equity funds to be invested. They have found that venture capital funds need longer to be fully invested than private equity funds. Moreover, they have found that when debt becomes more expensive, which is measured by the corporate bond yield, funds are invested more slowly. In addition, when competition for deal flows increases, which is captured by the total funds raised by competing funds, the time to be fully invested shortens.

Summary

This chapter has discussed sources of heterogeneity regarding private equity companies and their fundraising behaviour. Heterogeneity of private equity companies seems to be a key element in understanding European private equity industries especially with respect to investment patterns, to which I turn in the next chapter. Several sources of heterogeneity have been discussed. One source stresses the role of European governments in supporting and subsidizing private equity industries. Another source stresses the role of capital providers for the investment behaviour of private equity companies. Besides the heterogeneity, the relationship between capital providers and private equity companies has been discussed. The contractual design between them aims at mitigating problems of excessive risk taking by private equity companies, and by stimulating the intensity of monitoring and management support services provided by private equity companies to portfolio firms.

4
Investing

This chapter deals with the investing behaviour of private equity companies in portfolio firms. Investing is the second phase in the venture capital cycle, and this phase is more complex and lasts longer than the fundraising and exiting phase. In this phase, private equity companies select promising portfolio firms, they invest money in these firms, and they add their particular services to these firms. At the same time, private equity companies follow particular portfolio strategies in order to control portfolio risks and to increase portfolio returns.

The first part of this chapter describes particular characteristics of portfolio firms, such as the industries in which European private-equity-backed firms operate and the firms' development stages when receiving private equity finance. The second part discusses the relationship between venture capital and private equity companies and the portfolio firms in the light of problems stemming from asymmetric information about the quality of the firms' business ideas and their future profitability. The third part summarizes what is known about the hypothesis on the value that venture capital and private equity companies add to their portfolio firms. The fourth part describes and discusses investment strategies of private equity companies that they use to improve the return-risk profile of portfolios.

Firms receiving private equity finance

Three characteristics of firms receiving private equity finance are discussed in the following; the industry in which firms operate that received private equity finance, the development stages of these firms, and the geographical location of these firms.

Industry focus

Private equity investments concentrate on only a few industries as compared to all the industries available in a country. This is likely to be the result of the firm characteristics in these industries, returns on investments and exit possibilities for private equity companies. Because the involvement of venture capital companies in the form of monitoring and management support is time-consuming and therefore expensive compared to other sources of finance, only particular firms are interested in financing their investments with private equity. Private equity finance, and especially venture capital finance, is likely to be demanded more often in those industries characterized by a high degree of asymmetric information, asset intangibility and investment uncertainty. These characteristics make traditional financing forms very limited in scope. From the private equity companies' point of view, the potential for them to realize high returns when exiting from their participations causes them to focus on particular industries.

In order to give an impression of which industries European private equity companies invest in, I used the EVCA statistics, which distinguish 17 industries. Investment data for these industries are, however, not available for all countries and years. Therefore, I aggregated the data for the following seven industries: investments in communications, computers and other electronics (IT); investments in biotechnology and medicine (BIO); investments in energy (ENERGY); investments in agriculture and consumer-related products (AGRICULTURE); investments in transportation and industrial products (TRANSPORTATION); investments in chemicals and materials (CHEMICAL); and investments in industrial automation (IA).

Table 4.1 reports the percentage shares of private equity invested in these industries for European countries. The data reported are averages for the years 1991 to 2003. According to the shares averaged over European countries, the IT industry received more than 30 per cent of the private equity invested in Europe, followed by the AGRICULTURE industry and the TRANSPORTATION industry. Less than 11 per cent of the total private equity went into the BIO industry, and even less than 5 per cent went into the ENERGY, CHEMICAL, and IA industries.

Across countries, private equity companies invested with varying intensities in these industries. In Ireland, private equity companies invested more than 50 per cent of the private equity in the IT industry, while in Italy and Spain they invested only about 20 per cent of the private equity in this industry. In Denmark they invested almost 20 per cent in the BIO industry, while in Greece they invested less than 5 per cent in this

Table 4.1 Allocation of private equity across industries
This table reports investments in particular industries as a percentage of private equity investments, averaged over the years 1991 to 2003. IT denotes investments in communications, computers and other electronics. BIO denotes investments in biotechnology and medicine. ENERGY denotes investments in energy. AGRICULTURE denotes investments in agriculture and the consumer-related industry. TRANSPORTATION denotes investments in transportation and industrial products. CHEMICAL denotes investments in chemicals and materials. IA denotes investments in industrial automation. Time trend is the coefficient of a time trend in a fixed effects model including year dummies, where the endogenous variable is the share of investments in a particular industry. *** (*,+) denotes significance at the 1 (10, 15) per cent level.

	IT	BIO	ENERGY	AGRICULTURE	TRANSPORTATION	CHEMICAL	IA
Austria	41.45	12.00	0.13	9.66	33.27	0.61	2.86
Belgium	38.46	14.55	3.14	17.93	17.28	6.81	1.83
Denmark	38.52	19.64	0.65	6.33	28.08	4.00	2.78
Finland	40.93	13.57	2.86	16.12	18.19	7.32	1.01
France	27.03	10.35	1.11	29.92	27.33	2.85	1.41
Germany	26.94	11.39	0.46	12.26	36.05	11.14	1.75
Greece	32.74	4.93	0.05	52.14	7.41	0.89	1.85
Ireland	55.84	5.78	0.80	27.00	7.40	2.85	0.32
Italy	20.79	6.54	3.25	34.79	26.41	4.62	3.60
Netherlands	31.01	8.94	1.08	22.78	33.04	1.99	1.17
Norway	43.51	10.36	12.80	16.45	15.86	0.12	0.90
Portugal	25.89	6.58	5.42	29.86	26.67	4.74	0.84
Spain	14.32	5.39	5.04	42.70	23.57	8.31	0.67
Sweden	21.02	15.50	2.11	21.06	22.55	8.83	8.94
Switzerland	31.30	18.42	3.02	17.58	18.18	5.20	6.29
United Kingdom	23.01	10.86	2.67	39.10	18.97	4.15	1.24
Total	31.90	10.98	2.90	24.48	22.70	4.68	2.36
Time trend	1.39***	0.43+	−0.28	−0.69+	−0.76*	−0.02	−0.07

Source: EVCA (various issues), own calculations.

industry. In Norway they invested as much as 13 per cent in the ENERGY industry, while in many other countries they invested less than 1 per cent in this industry. In Greece they invested more than 50 per cent of the private equity in the AGRICULTURE industry, while in Denmark they invested only 6 per cent in this industry. In Germany they invested as much as 36 per cent of the private equity in the TRANSPORTATION industry, while in Greece and Ireland they invested only about 7 per cent in this industry. Moreover, in Germany they invested as much as 11 per cent in the CHEMICAL industry, while in Austria, Greece and Norway they invested less than 1 per cent. In Sweden they invested almost 9 per cent in the IA industry, while in many other countries they invested less than 2 per cent in this industry.

Thus, in Europe, private equity investments varied substantially with respect to the industries financed with private equity. This raises the question whether the allocation of private equity across industries and the industrial structure of European countries are linked. In Chapter 7, I will come back to this question by discussing whether private equity investments are related to the countries' comparative advantages in selected industries.

In order to give an impression of private equity investments in particular industries over time, I ran fixed-effects regressions including a time trend where the endogenous variable is the share of private equity invested in a particular industry. According to the coefficients of the time trend reported in Table 4.1, private equity investments in the IT industry and the BIO industry increased during the 1990s, while private equity investments in the AGRICULTURE industry and the TRANSPORTATION industry declined significantly over time.

Differences in the distribution of private equity across industries can be partly explained by the presence of various types of private equity companies, and by the presence of various types of capital providers. For the United States, Hellmann *et al.* (2004) have found evidence that bank-dependent private equity companies offer capital to those firms that are more likely to demand loans in their later stages of development. Because the loan demand may vary across industries, bank-dependent companies may not likewise finance firms operating in the industries in which independent private equity companies prefer to invest. Using the EVCA statistics, Schertler (2005a) has found evidence that new funds provided by pension funds, banks and governments have been more intensively used for investments in firms operating in the BIO industry than for investments in IT firms. In addition, using micro-data for private equity companies, Mayer *et al.* (2005) have found evidence that private equity companies that raise funds from pension funds favour investing in the BIO industry more often than the IT industry.

Stage focus

Apart from industry structure, a second characteristic of private equity industries is the allocation of investments across development stages of portfolio firms. The EVCA statistics distinguish several development stages, such as the early stage, the expansion stage, and later stages. In the early stage, the initial business concept is formed and prototypes of products are developed and compared with competing products in the market. Moreover, production is set up and an initial marketing campaign is launched, the market reaction to which is carefully analysed. By contrast, in the expansion stage, firms require large amounts of external financing because the cashflow often does not yet generate enough liquidity for the internal financing of the firms' growth. Because of this, the average volume of investments in the early stage of firms' development is expected to be lower than the volume in the expansion stage of firms' development. In the later stage, firms may require capital in crisis situations, for the acquisition of an existing firm by its own management (management buy-out) and for the takeover of privately held firms (management buy-in).

For investors, the risk of losing an investment decreases with firms' progress through the development stages. The risk of losing an investment spent in firms in the early stage of development, that is, before production is started, is over 60 per cent (Ruhnka and Young 1987). Internal factors, such as developing a prototype that does not work, predominantly give rise to this risk. External factors, such as unanticipated competition, constantly affect the risk over the development stages of firms; the impact only increases in the exiting phase, in which private equity companies sell the shares they held in portfolio firms to other shareholders (Ruhnka and Young 1991).

Not only is the risk of failure very high in the early stage, but firms in the early stage are also likely to have less collateral than firms in the expansion stage because they invest more often in intangible assets (Goel and Hasan 2004). In addition, evaluating the risks and returns of early-stage investments is likely to be more difficult than evaluating the risks and returns of later-stage investments. Investments in the early stage of portfolio firms are often seen as more important than investments in the later stages of firms' development because of the prominent role that young fast-growing firms are likely to play for economic growth (OECD 2002a).

Table 4.2 reports the percentages of private equity invested in the various development stages for European countries. The data reported are averages for the years 1991 to 2003. Again, there are differences between the European countries. In Finland, private equity companies invested as much as 30 per cent of the private equity in firms that were in the early stage of development, while in the United Kingdom they invested less than 5 per cent in this development stage. In Norway they invested almost 80 per cent of the private equity in firms that were in the expansion stage, while in Sweden and the United Kingdom they invested less than 30 per cent. In Sweden and the United Kingdom private equity companies invested more than 60 per cent of the private equity in management buy-outs, while in Greece and Norway they invested less than 5 per cent.

Combining the differences in the allocation of private equity across stages presented in Table 4.2, and the differences in the economic importance of private equity investments presented in Table 2.2 indicates significant differences in the financing of firms in the early and expansion stage of development that is often used as an approximation for venture capital activity in Europe. Explaining the level of venture capital and private equity activity will be at the centre of Chapter 6, which analyses empirically the determinants of cross-country variations in early-stage, expansion-stage and private equity investments.

Table 4.2 Allocation of private equity across development stages
This table reports investments in particular development stages as a percentage of private equity investments, averaged over the years 1991 to 2003. Time trend is the coefficient of a time trend in a fixed effects model including year dummies, where the endogenous variable is the share of investments in a particular development stage. *** denotes significance at the 1 per cent level.

	Early-stage	Expansion-stage	Buy-out
Austria	22.66	65.56	11.78
Belgium	24.82	60.64	14.54
Denmark	25.46	62.01	12.53
Finland	30.31	46.68	23.02
France	10.19	42.24	47.57
Germany	17.62	51.90	30.48
Greece	28.67	68.83	2.49
Ireland	20.21	67.10	12.69
Italy	11.95	45.01	43.04
Netherlands	14.04	51.07	34.90
Norway	16.77	79.48	3.75
Portugal	17.24	69.77	12.99
Spain	13.01	68.43	18.56
Sweden	8.49	28.71	62.80
Switzerland	18.07	46.00	35.93
United Kingdom	4.67	26.46	68.87
Total	17.55	54.72	27.73
Time trend	0.28	–2.57***	2.28***

Source: EVCA (various issues), own calculations.

In order to give an impression of private equity investments in particular stages over time, I ran fixed-effects regressions including a time trend. The estimation results reported in Table 4.2 show that the share of private equity invested in the early stage of firms' development did not change over time. By contrast, the share of private equity invested in firms' expansion stage declined significantly, while the share of private equity invested in management buy-out activities increased significantly over time. Thus, a significant part of the boom in Europe's private equity industries might be caused by the increase in management buy-outs.

Differences in the allocation of private equity across the various stages of firms' development can also be explained by the presence of various types of private equity companies, and by the presence of various types of capital providers. For the United States, Hellmann *et al.* (2004) have found evidence that bank-dependent private equity companies invest less frequently in the early stage than independent private equity companies do. Using the EVCA statistics, Schertler (2005a) has found evidence that new funds provided by academic institutions, pension funds and insurance companies affect the ratio of early-stage to later-stage investments positively, while new funds provided by banks and governments affect this ratio negatively. In addition, Mayer *et al.* (2005) have found evidence that private equity companies receiving capital from banks are more likely to invest in the later stage of firms' development.

Moreover, early-stage investments might be affected by the investments of business angels because business angel finance is likely to be complementary to venture capital finance. Business angels, who are often wealthy individuals, invest their own financial resources in firms' early stage of development. The effect of business angels' investments on venture capital investments depends on whether they are a close substitute for formal venture capital investments in the early stage of firms' development, or whether it is complementary to formal venture capital investments, in form of, for example, sequential investing and co-investments (Harrison and Mason 2000). In the first case, low levels of formal early-stage investments may result from high levels of business angel investments. In the latter case, however, low formal early-stage investments may result from low business angel investments.

The investments of business angels have been at the focus of recent literature. However, estimates given therein can only approximate the investments, since official statistics are not available. In the United States, business angels are estimated to invest about $60 billion annually (Van Osnabrugge and Robinson 2000). In the United Kingdom, it is estimated to be about ten times higher than the early-stage investments provided by formal venture capital companies (EBAN 1998). In Germany, 27,000 business angels were thought to provide annual investments amounting to about DM1.4 billion in the mid-1990s (Just 2000). Thus, business angel investments in the United States relative to GDP are four times as large as in the United Kingdom, which are in turn three times as large as in Germany. This is in line with the existence of complementarities between business angel investments and formal venture capital investments, so that low business angel investments are likely to be associated with low formal early-stage investments.

Regional focus

Apart from the concentration of private equity finance on a few industries and stages, private equity and especially venture capital finance is also concentrated regionally for several reasons (Dohse and Schertler 2004). First, venture capital companies are located in regions with sufficient investment opportunities. Because the transaction costs of actively providing management support and engaging in monitoring depend on the distance between venture capital companies and their portfolio firms, venture capital companies prefer to be located near their portfolio firms. Second, venture capital companies build networks to other venture capital companies and industrialists, leading to economies of scale. Network contacts to other venture capital companies are important in order to syndicate investments, that is, to finance a single firm through several venture capital companies, which can serve to engender information sharing (Bygrave and Timmons 1992) and to increase the experience of private equity companies in financing firms (Lerner 1994a). In addition, venture capital companies use network contacts to industrialists to set up contacts between their portfolio firms and their future customers and suppliers. For flourishing network contacts to develop, personal contacts that favour a regional concentration of venture capital finance may be important.

Private equity investments in Europe are concentrated, but less so than venture capital investments in the United States. For Germany, Holi *et al.* (2005) have reported that 27 per cent of all private equity companies are located in Bavaria, especially in Munich, and 19 per cent are located in North Rhine-Westphalia. According to Tejada (2003a), 80 per cent of the total private equity investments in Spain have been invested in Madrid, Cataluna and the Basque Country. For Portugal, Tejada (2003b) has reported that 50 per cent of the total investments have been invested in the Lisbon area. Of all the private equity investments in Norway, 90 per cent have been invested in the South East and Oslo (Baygan 2003b). Concerning Sweden, Baygan (2003c) has reported that the majority of private-equity-backed firms are located in Stockholm. For the United Kingdom, Baygan (2003a) has reported that the 52 per cent of the total investments have been invested in the South East and London. The regional concentration is not identical as regards to firms' development stages. In the United Kingdom, later-stage investments have been more relevant in those regions not in the centre (Mason and Harrison 2002).

Concerning Germany, Engel (2002) has analysed the regional distribution of private equity investments empirically. He has documented that private-equity-backed firms are located in urban districts in which a great number of new innovative ideas can be generated. He has found evidence that private equity flows to those regions that participated in the BioRegio contest. The German government launched the BioRegio contest, which aimed at supporting the development of biotechnology research (Engel 2002) and at developing regional concepts of the potential for commercializing the biotechnology industry within the German regions. Of the 17 regions that participated in this contest, the regions Munich, Rhineland (Wuppertal-Düsseldorf-Cologne-Aachen) and the Rhein-Neckar-Dreieck won and received DM150 million for supporting the biotechnology industry. In addition, firms in these regions that applied for funding under the German biotechnology programme, which invested up to DM1.5 billion between 1997 and 2001, have been evaluated favourably (Dohse 2000).

The relationship to portfolio firms

Young high-technology firms seeking finance differ from established firms in several aspects (see, for example, Lülfesmann 2000). First, the success of investments in young high-technology firms is very uncertain. Second, the founders of high-technology firms have excellent knowledge about their business idea but not necessarily about how to make money from it. Third, founders are wealth-constrained and therefore seek external finance. Because of these characteristics, the mechanisms used in the relationship between the founders of high-technology firms seeking finance and venture capital companies offering financial means, monitoring and management support services are highly complex.

The relationship between venture capital companies and their portfolio firms involves a selection stage and an investment stage. In the selection stage, venture capital companies carefully scrutinize the founders of firms and their business concepts before deciding whether to invest in the firms. In the investment stage, the venture capital companies invest capital in and monitor and support the progress of the portfolio firms.

In each of the two stages, severe problems, such as adverse selection and moral hazard, can arise between firms seeking the finance and the venture capital companies. These problems, and mechanisms to solve or mitigate these problems, will be discussed in the following. I start by discussing how venture capital companies solve adverse selection problems. Thereafter, I discuss how venture capital companies mitigate moral hazard problems. This section includes an analysis of incentive mechanisms used in the relationship between venture capital companies and portfolio firms from a theoretical and empirical point of view. Whenever it is possible, I present empirical evidence on the mechanisms used in Europe.

Adverse selection

Venture capital companies know neither the quality of the investment project nor the experience of the entrepreneur in developing business ideas. This asymmetric distribution of information before the investment decision is made can lead to adverse selection: venture capital companies want to select high-quality firms but they may select low-quality firms because they cannot distinguish between high-quality and low-quality firms. As in Akerlof's (1970) model of the automobile industry, Amit *et al.* (1990) have shown that under certain assumptions an ex-ante information asymmetry can lead to the non-existence of venture capital finance because the price of financing the most promising firms is too high. In order to reduce this information asymmetry, venture capital companies screen the founders and their business concepts carefully (Fried and Hisrich 1994). This is called deal screening.

Deal screening by venture capital companies and the origination of deals between venture capital and private equity companies and portfolio firms differs between countries because deal screening and origination are strongly affected by the country-specific legality conditions, as the empirical study by Cumming *et al.* (2004) indicates. Using an international dataset containing 3,828 private equity investments from 39 countries (from North and South America, Europe and Asia) over 32 years (1971–2003),[9] they have found evidence that a typical improvement in a legality index from 20 to 21 for developed nations lowers the time between receiving a business proposal and the actual investment decision by about 16 per cent.

Besides carefully screening investment opportunities, venture capital companies can employ several mechanisms that are specified in the contract between venture capital companies and portfolio firms to reduce the possibility of adverse selection (Houben and Nippel 2005). Venture capital companies can use entrepreneurs' compensation systems in order to minimize problems of adverse selection (Barry 1994). Tying the entrepreneurs' compensation to firm value can be interpreted as a mechanism with which venture capital companies can select the most promising firms, since, given this form of compensation, entrepreneurs do not prefer venture capital finance when their firms have dismal growth prospects (Weimerskirch 1998).

Other covenants to reduce the possibility of adverse selection are liquidation rights and rights to profits. With these tools, the profits of portfolio firms are distributed in a way more favoured by venture capital companies. Specifically, in the case of liquidation rights, the venture capital company has the preferred access to profits if a portfolio firm is liquidated or sold. With rights to profits, venture capital companies receive a fixed interest payment, which are often paid when the venture capital company exits. Therefore, rights to profits do not necessarily lower liquidity in the portfolio firms. Both tools lower entrepreneurs' expected pay-offs. Therefore, entrepreneurs that have investment projects with dismissal growth prospects have lower incentives to demand venture capital finance when venture capital companies employ liquidation rights and rights to profits. Bottazzi *et al.* (2004b), whose study uses an European sample of private equity companies, have reported that in 33 per cent of the cases analysed, private equity companies have liquidation rights, and in 43 per cent of the cases, private equity companies have rights to profits.[10]

Specifying liquidation preferences can make additional clauses in the contracts necessary. The liquidation preferences of venture capital companies or other agents involved in the portfolio firm may influence the decision of the portfolio firm to go public. Some owners of liquidation preferences might not be willing to give up this preference and this may, in extreme cases, hinder the going-public of the firm (Houben and Nippel 2005). Therefore, in the United States the contract parties often specify in the financing contract that convertible preferred equity is automatically converted into common stocks at the time of the initial public offering (Gompers 1997).

Not only may venture capital companies have limited information on entrepreneurs but entrepreneurs may also have limited information on venture capital companies. For entrepreneurs it is most important to have a basic understanding of what venture capital companies do. Gorman and Sahlman (1989) have described three critical services provided by venture capital companies. Venture capital companies build the investor group, review and help to formulate the business strategies, and fill the management teams. MacMillan *et al.* (1989) have described four critical services: development and operations, management selection, personnel management, and financial management. Entrepreneurs need to know that venture capital companies will not be involved in the day-to-day operations of their portfolio firms. Instead, they should expect that venture capital companies perform a specialized monitoring role (Wright and Robbie 1998). In the United Kingdom, the leading private equity company, which is likely to take on the support of the portfolio firms when several private equity companies invest money, usually contacts their portfolio firms by post or telephone more frequently than every fortnight (Wright and Lockett 2003). Leading private equity companies bring more skills with them to identify, screen and monitor portfolio firms than non-lead private equity companies (Lockett and Wright 1999).

But entrepreneurs not only need to know how venture capital finance works in general, they also need to know how a particular venture capital or private equity company operates. Entrepreneurs are not likely to know the intensity and quality of critical services provided by venture capital companies. This gives rise to an additional source of adverse selection in private equity industries. Several empirical studies have documented that private equity companies vary substantially in the intensity and quality of the critical services they provide (MacMillan *et al.* 1989, Gorman and Sahlman 1989, Sapienza 1992). For example, Elango *et al.* (1995) have reported that the most active group in their sample spent more than 35 hours per month per portfolio firm, while the least active group spends less than seven hours.

The intensity of management support differs with the types of private equity companies. For Germany, Zemke (1995) has found evidence that independent private equity companies support the management teams of the portfolio firms more intensively than their dependent counterparts when strategic decisions must be made in the portfolio firms. MBGs often do not offer consulting services that go beyond traditional arm's-length board activity (Wupperfeld 1994), while German savings-bank-dependent companies generally provide limited management support and monitoring (Kulicke 2001). Using micro-data from private equity companies located in the United States, the United Kingdom, the Netherlands, France and Belgium, Manigart *et al.* (2002) have found evidence that the intensity of management support provided by private equity companies is higher when they are independent from the capital providers. Using micro-data from the European Union, Norway and Switzerland, Bottazzi *et al.* (2004a, 2005) have found evidence that independent private equity companies are more involved in their portfolio firms than either corporate or bank-dependent or government-based private equity companies.

The study by Bottazzi *et al.* (2004a) has also shown that the likelihood of private equity companies' involvement in the portfolio firms depends on specialization, personal capacities, and human capital endowments. Regarding specialization, companies that do only venture capital deals are more often involved than companies that also do management buy-out deals. Regarding personal capacities, those private equity companies with a relatively low number of deals per partner are more likely to be involved in the portfolio firms than private equity companies with a higher number. And regarding human capital endowments, private equity companies whose partners have more business experience are more often involved in their portfolio firms. In addition, private equity companies whose partners have an education in science are less often involved in their portfolio firms.

Therefore, it is important for entrepreneurs to gather information on the intensity and quality of private equity companies' monitoring and supporting services and capacities.

Moral hazard

Moral hazard denotes a change in the behaviour of one contract party after the contract has been signed, and this change harms the other contract party. In the relationship between the venture capital companies and the portfolio firms, several types of moral hazard are possible: the portfolio firm decides to increase its research activities and to decrease its advertising efforts and this harms the venture capital company; the portfolio firm invests the capital provided in a riskier way than initially intended; the venture capital company decides to reduce management support in the form of, for example, networking or consultancy services and this harms the entrepreneur in the portfolio firm. As in the case of venture capital companies and capital providers discussed in the last chapter, the contract and the style of the relationship between the venture capital companies and portfolio firms is designed to mitigate these various types of moral hazard problems.

Generally, the monitoring services conducted by venture capital companies tend to lessen moral hazard behaviour of the portfolio firms (Sapienza *et al.* 1996). For the United States, several studies have documented the impact of venture capital backing on the corporate governance systems of the portfolio firms (Gompers 1995, Sahlman, 1990, Hellmann and Puri 2002). The change in these systems may ease venture capital companies' monitoring. There is also some evidence for Europe. Using a hand-collected dataset for Belgian firms, Beuselinck *et al.* (2004) have found evidence that private equity companies' involvement affects the ex-post financial reporting behaviour of the portfolio firms, which may improve the effectiveness of private equity companies' monitoring.

In order to monitor the portfolio firms but also to support them, private equity companies are often on the board of directors. Evidence based on US datasets indicates that venture capital has a significant effect on the size of the board of directors (Lerner 1995, Baker and Gompers 1999). Evidence based on European datasets indicates that the board representation of private equity companies depends on several factors. According to the study by Bottazzi *et al.* (2004a), the likelihood of private equity companies sitting on boards increases with the business experience and education in sciences of the private equity companies' partners. Moreover, the likelihood of sitting on the board of directors is significantly higher for independent private equity companies, for younger private equity companies, for private equity companies managing smaller funds, and for private equity companies that invest only in venture capital deals but not in management buy-out deals. Using an international dataset, Cumming *et al.* (2004) have found that the likelihood of private equity companies being represented on boards increases by more than 4 per cent when the legality index improves from 20 to 21, which it typically does as regards developed nations.

The venture capital company increases the portfolio firm's incentives to exert high efforts by compensating the entrepreneur of the portfolio firm in a manner that is incentive-increasing. An incentive-increasing compensation involving basic salaries and profit participation not only reduces adverse selection problems but offers the entrepreneur of the portfolio firm strong incentives to add his/her specific technological expertise in the development of the business idea and also in the commercialization of the product after the contract has been signed.

Moreover, the venture capital company increases the entrepreneur's incentives to exert high efforts by investing capital in stages. The staging of investment offers the venture capital company the opportunity to abandon the investment after each capital infusion if contractually specified financial or non-financial criteria, so-called milestones, are not met (Sahlman 1990).[11] This sets strong incentives for entrepreneurs to exert high effort and to avoid high risks. In addition, this staging of investment offers the entrepreneur the opportunity to use other financial resources after each capital infusion (Smith 1999). However, the infusion of capital in stages can cause disincentives as well. Cornelli and Yosha (2003) have shown theoretically that an entrepreneur has incentives to manipulate short-term performance of the portfolio firm when capital is invested in stages. In their model, convertible securities are used to counteract this disincentive.

In addition to the one-sided moral hazard problems already mentioned, the recent theoretical literature has discussed double-sided moral hazard problems in venture capital finance (Repullao and Suarez 2004, Casamatta 2003, Lülfesmann 2000, Houben 2003, Schmidt 2003). These models build on the observation that venture capital companies offer several support services apart from monitoring the portfolio firms: they offer contacts to other market participants such as customers and suppliers. They offer contacts to their networks that allow key managers for the portfolio firm to be recruited more effectively. Because of these services, a situation is assumed in the theoretical models in which the expected pay-off of the firm depends on the value-increasing effort of the entrepreneur as well as on the value-increasing effort of the venture capital company. Some models show, under certain circumstances, that the value-increasing effort of both parties is too low in equilibrium in the case of pure equity contracts. However, the value-increasing efforts of both parties are optimal in the case of convertible securities.

Bascha and Walz (2002a) have argued that convertible securities are also used to mitigate agency problems arising at the time of the exit of the venture capital company. Bascha and Walz (2002b) have documented weak evidence that collaborates their arguments. In their analysis they used data on private equity companies' portfolios, not on individual deals. Based on 47 observations, they have found evidence that the percentage of convertible securities used in private equity companies' portfolios increases with the expected amount of initial public offerings, while it declines with the expected amount of trade sales. They have also documented that private equity companies with high return demands use significantly more convertible securities.

According to a study by Schwienbacher (2002), who has analysed private equity companies operating in Europe and the United States, convertible securities are much more often used in the United States than in European countries. Kaplan and Strömberg (2003) have documented that in 189 of 200 US venture capital financing rounds they analysed, convertible preferred stocks are used. Gilson and Schizer (2002) have argued that convertible securities are favoured in the United States because of a tax bias in favour of convertible securities. In a sample of German private equity companies, Bascha and Walz (2002b) have found that besides using silent partnerships, private equity companies more often use pure equity, and less frequently use convertible securities. Thirty three per cent of the 60 private equity companies in their sample use silent partnerships, almost 27 per cent use pure equity, while only about 11 per cent use convertible securities.[12]

Hypothesis on value-added

As documented in the last part, venture capital companies provide several services to their portfolio firms. Whether these services matter for the performance of the portfolio firms cannot be analysed easily because performance measures of portfolio firms are not available. Therefore, other measures such as employment growth, behaviour in product markets, and patenting behaviour are focused by researchers asking whether venture capital backing increases the performance of portfolio firms, that is, whether venture capital companies add value to their portfolio firms.

Evidence based on US datasets indicates that venture capital has a significant effect on the performance of venture-capital-backed firms. Venture capital backing affects significantly the position of the firm in the product market (Hellmann and Puri 2000), its patenting behaviour (Kortum and Lerner 2000), its performance after the initial public offering (Brav and Gompers 1997), the timing of the initial public offering (Lerner 1994b) and the costs when the firm goes to a public equity market (Megginson and Weiss 1991).

Evidence based on European datasets has grown substantially in recent years, especially because several datasets have been constructed to analyse venture capital and private equity industries. However, studies based on European datasets have clear limits for at least four reasons.

First, the number of observations is quite often very small and there is severe concern regarding selection bias in many datasets. Second, the majority of studies use data from the end of the 1990s and this raises concerns about the general validity of estimation results. Thus, results are only based on a period of higher stock prices of high-technology firms. Third, the time frame of these datasets is too short to capture industry cycle effects. Capturing industry cycle effects may be very important when analysing the value that venture capital companies add to their portfolio firms, since the value-added is likely to be less pronounced in industry boom phases. Kanniainen and Keuschnigg (2004), who have analysed the portfolios of venture capital companies theoretically, have argued that monitoring and management support is affected by supply and demand conditions. If the venture capital industry expands, the number of experienced managers of venture capital funds cannot be increased in the short run, therefore management support per portfolio firm is reduced in the short run. Fourth, studies do not always take into account the heterogeneity of private equity companies in Europe. Taking into account the various types of private equity companies and their level of experience is important, since the quality and intensity of management support and monitoring services differ among various types and levels of experience, and so does the value-added. Tykvova (2004) has argued that independent and corporate private equity companies are likely to create a higher value-added in the portfolio firms than bank-dependent or government-based private equity companies. This is because independent and corporate private equity companies offer not only capital but also management support and advice, whereas bank-dependent and government-based private equity companies are typically only bridge investors.

Several empirical studies based on the available European datasets point out that there is no significant link between private equity backing and employment growth in the portfolio firms while others point out that there is a significant link. Using survey data for 500 German and British high-technology firms Bürgel *et al.* (2000) have found neither a significant impact of private equity backing on employment growth nor of private equity backing on sales growth. Using a European dataset for initial public offerings, Bottazzi and Da Rin (2002a) have found no link between private equity backing and employment growth. In contrast, for German Neuer Markt firms, Audretsch and Lehmann (2002) have found that private-equity-backed firms realize higher growth rates in employment than non-private-equity-backed firms. For 300 private-equity-backed firms in Denmark,

Christensen and Christensen (2003) have found a significant link between private equity backing and employment growth but not between private equity backing and revenue growth.

These studies indicate that there might be a positive relationship between private equity backing and the performance of the private-equity-backed firms. However, these studies do not allow an assessment of whether the positive relationship stems from the selection process of the private equity companies (private-equity-backed firms are a positively selected group, which cannot simply be compared with a group of non-private-equity-backed firms) or whether it stems from private equity companies' capital supply and their monitoring and supporting services during the investment stage. The study by Engel (2003a) has distinguished these two effects by using a matching algorithm of private-equity-backed and non-private-equity-backed firms. It has shown that Germany's private-equity-backed firms realize higher employment growth than comparable non-private-equity-backed firms. Engel (2003a) has calculated that private-equity-backed firms achieve, on average, 123 per cent points higher employment growth than their non-private-equity-backed counterparts. In this part of the study Engel has, however, not taken into account the heterogeneity of private equity companies. Moreover, in another part of the study, Engel (2003a) has found evidence that the employment growth of portfolio firms depends on the characteristics of private equity companies. More specifically, he has found that portfolio firms realize higher employment growth if their private equity company is regionally concentrated and has a higher level of experience.

The innovation activities of private-equity-backed firms have also been at the centre of empirical studies using European datasets. Engel and Keilbach (2002) have used a statistical matching procedure in order to analyse the innovation activities of young German firms. They have found evidence that innovative firms are more likely to receive private equity backing. After private equity infusion, private-equity-backed firms show higher growth rates but not higher innovation activities. They have argued that private equity companies in Germany help their portfolio firms to commercialize their products but not to innovate further. Unfortunately, Engel and Keilbach (2002) have not controlled for the different influences of various types of private equity companies active in the German market.

Another body of literature has analysed the impact of private equity backing on the *long-run performance* of firms after their initial public offering. For the United States, Brav and Gompers (1997) have found some evidence when using weighted returns that venture-capital-backed firms outperform non-venture-capital-backed firms after going public. Doukas and Gonenc (2001) have not found a significant link between venture capital backing and long-run performance. Using an initial public offering sample for the Neuer Markt, Rindermann (2003) has found that the stock market performance of firms backed by bank-dependent and independent private equity companies is better than it is with firms backed by government-based private equity companies. Using the Neuer Markt dataset, Tykvova and Walz (2004) have reported that post-IPO market performance is significantly better for those firms backed by independent private equity companies than for firms backed by bank- or government-dependent private equity companies or non-private-equity-backed firms. Using an argument developed by Neus and Walz (2005), Tykvova and Walz (2004) have also tested whether experienced private equity companies are able to price the firms in their portfolios more precisely, resulting in a lower volatility of returns after the initial public offering. Indeed, their empirical analysis has revealed that independent private equity companies do reduce firm-specific volatility in the aftermarket. Thus, backing by an independent private equity company not only affects returns but has also a significant impact on the risk captured by the volatility of returns.

Using the Neuer Markt IPO dataset, Tykvova (2004) has found evidence that independent private equity companies are more proficient in timing initial public offerings of portfolio firms than their dependent counterparts. Proficiency in the timing of initial public offering may help to reduce portfolio firms' cost when going public.

Portfolios strategies

Private equity companies do not only invest in one firm. They also build portfolios. Private equity companies can make use of two portfolio strategies in order to maximize returns on their portfolios for a given level of risks. First, they can specialize their investments in firms operating in particular industries and/or in firms in particular stages of development. Second, they can syndicate their investments. In a private equity syndicate, several private equity companies finance a single firm for a joint pay-off (Wilson 1968) and mainly one private equity company takes on the monitoring and support of the firm. In this part, I start by presenting data informing on the number of firms in portfolios of private equity companies. Then, I discuss the specialization in the portfolios of private equity companies. Finally, I discuss syndication activities of private equity companies.

Numbers of firms in portfolios

Kanniainen and Keuschnigg (2004) have analysed theoretically what determines the size of portfolios. They have argued that the optimal portfolio is determined by the trade-off between the number of portfolio firms that must be supported and by the level of management support per portfolio firm. Using data from a survey of various types of private equity funds in Europe and North America, Bernile *et al.* (2005) have analysed the portfolio size of private equity companies empirically. They have documented that the size of private equity companies' portfolios depends positively on the size of the fund raised.

Insights into the portfolio of private equity companies can be gained by using information on French and Germany private equity companies offered by the respective venture capital associations. German private equity companies have 38.5 firms, on average, in their portfolios. However, the distribution of portfolio firms among private equity companies is very unequal: The first quartile is 4.8, the median is 17.0, and the third quartile is as high as 114.0. More than 30 per cent of all private equity companies have fewer than ten firms in their portfolios; almost 60 per cent have fewer than 20 firms in their portfolios. Only seven private equity companies have more than 100 portfolio firms.

French private equity companies have, on average, 52 firms in their portfolios, 13 firms more than their German counterparts. More than 20 per cent of the French private equity companies have fewer than ten firms in their portfolios, and another 20 per cent have more than 100 firms in their portfolios. Thus, the distribution of portfolio firms among the French private equity companies' portfolios is rather unequal, similar to the German distribution. The median of the number of portfolio firms is as low as 27, while the third quartile is about 60.

One reason for the unequal distribution of portfolio firms might be the presence of various types of private equity companies in both markets. Indeed, in Germany, the number of portfolio firms of government-based private equity companies is substantially higher than the number of portfolio firms of any other type of private equity company. Both the average number, which is 144.4, and the median, which is 72.5, are much higher than the respective numbers for the other private equity companies. The *Mittelständische Beteiligungsgesellschaft Baden-Württemberg GmbH,* a government-based private equity company, has more than 900 portfolio firms. Compared with bank-dependent private equity companies, independent private equity companies seem to be more heterogeneous with respect to the number of portfolio firms, as mean and median values indicate. The reason for this might be that the number of portfolio firms of bank-dependent private equity companies can be interpreted as long-term averages, while the number of portfolio firms of independent private equity companies cannot because many of these companies were not founded until the end of the 1990s.

Distinguishing between the various types of private equity companies also helps in explaining the unequal distribution of portfolio firms in the portfolios of French private equity companies. With an average number of 72 and a median value of 44, bank-dependent private equity companies have a particularly large number of firms in their portfolios. Moreover, French bank-dependent private equity companies have considerably more firms in their portfolios than German bank-dependent private equity companies. Corporate private equity companies have fewer portfolio firms than bank-dependent companies, but more than independent private equity companies.

Interestingly, French independent private equity companies have 35 firms on average (median value is 17) in their portfolios, while the German independent companies only have 25 firms on average (median value is 11) in their portfolios. This difference can be explained by the fact that German independent companies are comparably young. About 50 per cent of the German independent companies have been established since 1998. In France, foundation data for 40 independent companies are available. Three independent private equity companies were founded in 2000, three in 1999, and two in 1998. Thus, 20 per cent of the French independent private equity companies may have been established in the last three years, while in Germany, 50 per cent of the independent private equity companies may have been established during the same period.

Specialization in portfolios

At any point in time, private equity companies have a multitude of firms in their portfolios. This raises the question of whether private equity companies have particular portfolio strategies such as portfolio diversification or portfolio specialization. Portfolio diversification means that private equity companies invest in a wide range of firms in different development stages and/or in different industries. Portfolio specialization means that they invest only in firms at particular development stages and/or in firms operating in particular industries. The portfolio specialization strategy is likely to lead to portfolios that are not well-diversified, that is, not all unsystematic risk is diversified away (Norton and Tenenbaum 1993).

However, portfolio specialization helps to gain a solid understanding of, and experience in, selected, often complex, industries (De Clercq and Sapienza 2004, Gupta and Sapienza 1992, Norton and Tenenbaum 1993). As Amit *et al.* (1998) have argued, portfolio specialization allows venture capital companies to build up a comparative advantage over other financial intermediaries in the selection and monitoring of high-technology firms. This strategy might help in mitigating the informational disadvantage that they have in comparison to those institutional investors investing in publicly quoted firms (Fama 1991). In the following, I first describe the specialization in the portfolios of private equity companies and then I discuss factors affecting specialization.

Empirical figures

The German and French VC datasets (which are based on surveys) inform on private equity companies' portfolio strategies. All specialization measures are based on the propensity of private equity companies to be willing to invest in particular firms, and not on the allocation of the portfolio across industries and development stages. Germany's private equity companies have a relatively low degree of specialization. Only around 38 per cent of all private equity companies are specialized either in a particular industry or in particular stages of firm development. Only about one-fifth of all private equity companies are specialized in particular industries and in particular stages. Compared to Germany's private equity companies, French private equity companies have a higher degree of specialization in particular stages, but not in particular industries. Only around 22 per cent of all private equity companies are specialized in particular industries, while almost 90 per cent are specialized in particular stages. Only about one-fifth of all French private equity companies are specialized in particular stages and at the same time in selected industries. Unfortunately, the stages of firms' development are defined slightly differently in the two datasets. In the German dataset, seven development stages are distinguished, while in the French dataset only five stages are distinguished.

Specialization in the particular stages and in selected industries differs considerably between the various types of private equity companies. In Germany, independent private equity companies have a considerably higher degree of specialization than bank-dependent and government-based companies with respect to industries and particular stages, as well as with respect to simultaneous specialization in particular industries and particular stages. French independent private equity companies, by contrast, do not show a much higher degree of specialization than their bank-dependent counterparts with respect to industries and particular stages. Almost 50 per cent of the independent private equity companies are specialized in financing firms operating in the biotechnology and medical industry and/or the communications and computer industry. Thirty eight per cent of the specialized bank-dependent private equity companies focus on financing firms operating in the biotechnology and medical industry, while almost 88 per cent focus on financing firms operating in the communications and computer industry.

In which industries and which stages of firms' development do German private equity companies specialize? Almost 70 per cent of all private equity companies that are industrially specialized indicate that they would invest in firms operating in the biotechnology and medical industry, while about 49 per cent would invest in firms operating in the communications and computer industry. About 60 per cent of the private equity companies that are specialized in particular stages of firms' development, invest their capital in the early stage and/or the expansion stage.

Almost every other French private equity company offers capital to firms that are in the early stage. In Germany, by contrast, more than 70 per cent of all private equity companies supply start-up capital. At the beginning of the early stage, private capital companies provide seed capital, while later on they provide start-up capital. Thus, as compared to their German counterparts, French private equity companies seem to be less willing to invest money in the firms' early stage. Three out of four French private equity companies are willing to invest in firms that are in their expansion stage (in which capital is required to finance the firms' growth), while in Germany nine out of ten private equity companies are willing to invest in these firms.

What about the supply of private equity for firms that are in the earliest stage of development? Forty per cent of all German private equity companies in the sample indicate that they would provide seed capital. More than 70 per cent of all private equity companies would provide start-up capital and almost 90 per cent would provide capital to firms that need money to finance their growth, since their cashflows are not sufficient to allow internal financing (these firms are in the expansion stage).

With respect to private equity companies' propensity to invest in firms' development stages, the differences between the four types of companies are also substantial. Bank-dependent private equity companies seem to be more risk-averse, since they shy away from providing seed capital. Only 19.4 per cent of bank-dependent private equity companies would provide seed capital, while almost 55 per cent would provide start-up capital. Compared to bank-dependent companies, government-based companies and savings-banks-dependent companies would provide capital more frequently for the firms' early stage. About 39 per cent of them would provide seed capital, while 78 (65) per cent of the government-based companies (savings-banks-dependent companies) would provide start-up capital. The independent private equity companies have a considerably higher share of private equity companies (50 per cent) that would provide seed capital than all other types of private equity companies.

The various types of French private equity companies do not differ considerably with respect to their willingness to finance firms' early stage of development. Moreover, the differences with respect to financing the expansion stage of firms' development also seems extremely moderate, while the differences between the four German types are substantial. While French bank-dependent companies and their independent counterparts have a similar propensity to invest in the expansion stage, German bank-dependent companies have a substantially lower propensity than their independent counterparts. Above all, German bank-dependent companies generally do not often finance the firms' early stage, while independent private equity companies have a rather high propensity to do so. The finding that bank-dependent companies invest less frequently in firms' early stage than other types of private equity companies do run counter to the result obtained by Mayer *et al.* (2005), who have found that bank-dependent private equity companies are as much involved in financing the firms' early stage as other private equity companies.

Factors determining specialization

So far, I have described only the private equity companies' specialization in industries and stages of firm development. In the following, I identify factors that drive specialization patterns. The degree of industrial and early-stage specialization in private equity companies' portfolios depends on several factors, as the evidence from the United States indicates. First, portfolio specialization varies with the type of venture capital companies. Corporate venture capital companies have a higher degree of specialization in industries than other venture capital companies, while small business investment companies[13] seem to have no preference regarding industry diversity (Gupta and Sapienza 1992). Second, venture capital companies managing large funds prefer greater industry diversity than venture capital companies managing small funds (Gupta and Sapienza 1992). Third, venture capital companies that focus on the early stage of firms' development are on average more specialized in particular industries than venture capital companies that focus on the later stages of firms' development (Norton and Tenenbaum 1993, Gupta and Sapienza 1992). US venture capital companies that are specialized in the early stage demand lower returns for early-stage investments than companies that are not (Manigart *et al.* 2002).

Thus, I tested whether the volume of funds under management and the type of the private equity company have a statistically significant impact on the specialization of European private equity companies by using the VCPro dataset. I calculated four measures that are related to the degree of specialization and used all of them as endogenous variables. The first measure I used is the number of industries, in which private equity companies have a propensity to invest. This variable is a count variable that takes values between one and 18. The second measure I used is the number of stages in which the private equity companies are willing to invest. This variable is also a count variable and takes values between one and 12. The third measure I used is industrial specialization, which is a dummy variable, and which equals one if private equity companies invest in not more than five industries, and zero otherwise. The fourth measure I used is early-stage specialization, which is a dummy variable, and which equals one if private equity companies are specialized in the early stage, and zero otherwise.[14]

Because the number of industries and stages in which private equity companies indicate they would invest are count variables, the classical linear regression model is inappropriate because the distribution of residuals is heteroscedastically non-normal and the predicted probabilities can take values above unity (Blundell *et al.* 1995). With count variables it has become common to apply a poisson or negative binomial (NEGBIN) model, following the seminal works by Gourieroux *et al.* (1984a,b), Hausman *et al.* (1984) and Cameron and Trivedi (1986). Because the NEGBIN model is more general than the poisson model, as it allows for heterogeneity in the mean function and thus relaxes the variance restriction, I used a NEGBIN model to analyse the number of industries and stages in which private equity companies have a propensity to invest.

Columns (2) and (3) in Table 4.3 report the estimation results for the number of industries, and the number of stages.[15] The number of industries in which a private equity company has a propensity to invest depends on the type of the private equity company and on the

Table 4.3 Specialization in industries and stages

This table reports estimation results for industrial and early-stage specialization. OLS: significance test is a F-test, R^2 is adjusted, and absolute t-statistics are given below the coefficients. NEGBIN and LOGIT: significance test is a χ^2-test, R^2 is pseudo, and absolute z-statistics are given below the coefficients. For the definition of variables see Table A2. *** (**,*) denotes significance at the 1 (5, 10) per cent level.

	(1) Average investment volume	(2) Number of industries	(3) Number of stages	(4) Industrial specialization	(5) Early-stage specialization
	OLS	NEGBIN	NEGBIN	LOGIT	LOGIT
Specialists	–21.360***	–0.271***	0.105***	0.781***	1.828***
	(4.08)	(5.83)	(2.72)	(3.4)	(5.05)
Government	–23.481***	0.073	0.208*	–1.448	1.933***
	(4.25)	(0.54)	(1.84)	(1.26)	(2.66)
Funds under management		0.000***	0	–0.001*	–0.002**
		(5.28)	(1.45)	(1.77)	(2.07)
Constant	12.731**	2.672***	0.713***	–1.752	–1.640**
	(2.44)	(13.8)	(6.85)	(1.44)	(2.37)
Number of observations	626	632	632	632	614
Significance test	3.551	143.2	61.112	45.65	61.451
R^2	0.059	0.023	0.013	0.102	0.164

Source: VCPro dataset, own calculations.

volume of funds under management. Specialists have a lower number of industries in which they are willing to invest, while government-based companies do not differ from generalists with respect to the number of industries. The number of stages in which a private equity company has a propensity to invest is statistically higher for specialists and government-based companies than for generalists. The number of stages does not depend on the volume of funds under management.

For industrial specialization and early-stage specialization, I used a binary choice model, since these variables are dummy variables that equal zero or one (Wooldridge 2002). Binary choice models specify the probability that a private equity company is specialized in particular industries or the early stage as a function of exogenous variables, such as the type of the private equity company, and the volume of funds under management.

Columns (4)–(5) in Table 4.3 report the estimation results for industrial specialization and early-stage specialization as endogenous variables. The results indicate that the type of the private equity company matters for industrial and early-stage specialization. Specialists are more often industrially specialized than generalists or government-based companies. Specialists and government-based companies are more often specialized in the early stage than generalists. The higher the volume of the funds under management is, the lower the likelihood that private equity companies are specialized in industries and the early stage.

To sum up, the industrial and the early-stage specialization of private equity companies in the United States and Europe is driven by similar factors. First, the estimations show that specialization depends on the type of the company. Second, specialization depends on the volume of funds under management.

Syndication

Another important portfolio strategy is the syndication of investments. Within venture capital and private equity syndicates, two or more private equity companies take an equity stake in portfolio firms (Manigart *et al.* 2004), narrowly defined a private equity syndicate is a syndicate in which the equity stakes are taken in the same investment round, while broadly defined it is a syndicate in which the equity stakes may have been taken in different investment rounds (Brander *et al.* 2002). In the following, I start by discussing the costs and benefits of syndications seen from the private equity companies' point of view. Then, I discuss the importance of syndication in

Europe, and the factors that determine the private equity companies' decision to syndicate an investment deal.

Costs and benefits

Syndication is not costless for several reasons. First, the private equity company that wants to syndicate an investment deal has to find an appropriate partner. Thus, there are costs involved in selecting a private equity company. These costs depend on whether the private equity company is involved in large and effective networks. For a well-established private equity company, selection costs might be rather low. Wright and Lockett (2003) have reported that private equity companies form repeated syndicates in different portfolio firms and that private equity companies are sometimes the lead and sometimes the follower or non-lead investor. Second, the decision-making within a syndicate is more expensive than the decision making of a private equity company in a standalone investment deal. This is because interests within the syndicate must be bundled and actions must be coordinated. Third, agency conflicts between members of a private equity syndicate can lead to severe agency costs (Fried and Hisrich 1994, Wright and Lockett 2003).

Syndication can be beneficial for the private equity company that wants to syndicate a deal for several reasons. First, private equity companies syndicate an investment deal in order to share risks on a deal-to-deal basis that could lead to a reduction of the overall portfolio risk without giving up returns (Manigart *et al.* 2002). This argument is especially strong for private equity companies specialized in firms in particular stages of development or industries. In addition, private equity companies syndicate in order to decrease liquidity risks. Since private equity companies invest in unlisted firms, their capital is bound for a longer period of time than if they would invest in listed firms. Private equity companies should strive to access a diversity of portfolio firms at the initial investment stage because these require lower amounts of investment (Lockett and Wright 1999).

Second, private equity and especially venture capital companies syndicate their investments to increase the resource pool which can be important in the selection stage, and the investment stage. Because venture capital companies operating in a syndicate evaluate a portfolio firm's proposal in the selection stage, the syndicate may reduce the potential danger of adverse selection (Lerner 1994a, Houben 2003). Combining the effort to assess the quality of a portfolio firm helps venture capital companies to overcome informational asymmetries. Informational asymmetries exist because the entrepreneurs typically know more about the investment opportunity they are seeking funding for and thus might overstate the attractiveness of their proposals (Sorenson and Stuart 2002).[16] Because venture capital companies operating in a syndicate support a portfolio firm in the investment stage, the syndicate may increase the performance of the portfolio firm more than a single venture capital company. This is, in turn, because the venture capital companies in a syndicate may have heterogeneous skills and network contacts that they add to the portfolio firm (Brander *et al.* 2002). The need for such additional resources is likely to be greater in the early stage of portfolio firms than in later stages. This is mainly due to the fact that more mature portfolio firms have already established a management structure and a market position and have already built up relationships with suppliers and customers in their industry (Lockett and Wright 1999, Brander *et al.* 2002).

Third, private equity companies may syndicate their investments in order to band together rather than to compete with other private equity companies. By banding together, private equity companies improve their market power *vis-à-vis* entrepreneurs seeking private equity finance.

Fourth, private equity companies syndicate in order to minimize agency conflicts (Admati and Pfleiderer 1994). In the model by Admati and Pfleiderer (1994), a venture capital company gets inside information on the portfolio firm by financing the first capital infusion. The authors have shown that the continuation decision of the lead venture capital company (which finances the first capital infusion) is optimal only if the venture capital company's share in expected revenue is equal to its initial investment share. Hence, capital infusions must be syndicated in order to ensure that the lead venture capital company has a constant share in the expected revenue.

Empirical figures

In order to describe the empirical relevance of syndicated investments in Europe, Table 4.4 provides information on the percentage of non-syndicated private equity investments, the percentage of domestically syndicated investments and the percentage of internationally syndicated investments. Data are averaged over the years 1991 to 2003. Overall, only 34 per cent of the total private equity investments were syndicated either domestically or internationally. The degree of syndication varied between the European countries. In some countries, such as France, Belgium and Switzerland, private equity companies syndicated almost or even more than 50 per cent of the private equity investments. In other countries, such as Ireland and Sweden they syndicated only 20 per cent of the private equity investments. In some countries the importance of nationally syndicated investments, compared to internationally syndicated investments, was astonishing. In Austria, for example, 13 per cent of the private equity investments were nationally syndicated, compared to 23 per cent of the private equity investments that were internationally syndicated. Since handling international syndicates is likely to be more expensive than national syndicates, one would expect the relevance of nationally syndicated investments to be higher than internationally syndicated investments. This holds for many but not for all of the countries under

Table 4.4 Syndication of investments
This table reports non-syndicated, domestically syndicated and internationally syndicated investments as a percentage of private equity investments, averaged over the years 1991 to 2003. Time trend is the coefficient of a time trend in a fixed effects model including year dummies, where the endogenous variable is the percentage of private equity investments that are either not syndicated or nationally syndicated or internationally syndicated. ** denotes significance at the 5 per cent level.

	Not-syndicated	Nationally syndicated	Internationally syndicated
Austria	63.90	12.82	23.28
Belgium	50.87	28.27	20.86
Denmark	62.02	26.42	11.56
Finland	74.37	19.76	5.87
France	43.70	36.65	19.65
Germany	56.53	36.17	7.30
Greece	77.81	12.93	9.26
Ireland	81.72	9.20	9.09
Italy	61.73	24.83	13.43
Netherlands	77.83	13.59	8.57
Norway	77.02	11.99	10.98
Portugal	59.37	35.99	4.64
Spain	78.56	13.03	8.41
Sweden	80.95	12.09	6.96
Switzerland	50.76	9.27	39.98
United Kingdom	61.59	25.50	12.91
Total	65.81	20.77	13.42
Time trend	–0.32	–0.52	0.85**

Source: EVCA (various issues), own calculations.

consideration. One explanation for this might be that international syndication is more important for small countries that are more likely to generate an insufficient deal flow for private equity companies.

A more detailed picture of syndication behaviour can be obtained from micro-data on private equity companies and private-equity-backed firms. Based on a micro-dataset of European private equity companies, Schwienbacher (2002) has reported that on average 54 per cent of the deals by the European private equity companies are syndicated. Moreover, European private equity companies have, on average, 2.7 partners. Government-based private equity companies are included in 12 per cent of the European private equity syndicates.

I extracted additional information on syndication behaviour in Germany and France from the IPO datasets of the Neuer Markt and the Nouveau Marché. These datasets are described in detail in the Appendix. In these datasets, I define syndication broadly, since I have no information on whether private equity companies decided about their investments in a portfolio firm at the same point in time. According to these datasets, private equity syndicates in Germany and France are as popular as in other European countries. Forty five per cent of the 146 private-equity-backed firms that went public on the Neuer Markt, and 56 per cent of the 66 private-equity-backed firms that went public on the Nouveau Marché were financed by more than one private equity company. Eighteen per cent of the private-equity-backed firms that went public on the Neuer Markt, and 30 per cent of the private-equity-backed firms that went public on the Nouveau Marché had more than two private equity companies. Large syndicates with more than five private equity companies were not very common. They accounted for only 1.4 per cent of the private-equity-backed firms that went public on the Neuer Markt and 3 per cent of the private-equity-backed firms that went public on the Nouveau Marché.

Syndication is a repeated game. Thirty five per cent of the total 65 syndicates in the Neuer Markt and 24 per cent of the total 37 syndicates of the Nouveau Marché invested together more than once. In the Neuer Markt sample, *Technologie-Beteiligungsgesellschaft mbH, Techno Venture Management GmbH* and *Alpinvest Int. B.V.* financed the portfolio firms *co.don* and *GPC Biotech*. The *Technologie-Beteiligungsgesellschaft,* the *IKB Beteiligungsgesellschaft* and *Atlas Venture* financed the portfolio firms *MediGene* and *GPC Biotech*. In the Nouveau Marché sample, for example, *Galileo* and *Apollo Invest* financed the portfolio firms *Aufeminin* and *KaZiBao*. *Galileo* and *Banexi Ventures* financed the portfolio firms *Emme* and *Genesys*.

Factors determining syndication

In order to gauge whether private equity companies bundle different skills in their syndicates which are likely to increase the value that private equity companies add to portfolio firms, I describe in the following whether private equity companies involved in the syndicates are similar with respect to three characteristics. These are the organizational type of the private equity companies, their specialization in various stages of firms' development, and their specialization in particular industries in which the portfolio firms they have financed operate. De Clercq and Dimov (2004) have argued that private equity companies that are more specialized in financing firms in selected industries or stages of development have a greater need to syndicate in order to get complementary skills necessary to succeed in the investment deal.

Regarding organizational type, I distinguish between five types of private equity companies: government-based companies, private bank-dependent companies, savings-bank-dependent companies, corporate private equity companies and independent private equity companies. In the Neuer Markt sample, there are only five syndicates existed that are composed of private equity companies whose organizational types are identical. Interestingly, four of them are independent private equity companies, and in one case the syndicate had only private bank-dependent companies. In the Nouveau Marché sample, there are six syndicates composed of private equity companies whose organizational type is identical. Four syndicates are composed of private bank-dependent companies, one is composed of independent private equity companies, and one is composed of corporate private equity companies only.

Regarding specialization in industries in which the portfolio firms operate, I created a dummy variable equal to one if the private equity company would invest in only a few industries, and zero otherwise. Unfortunately, the samples contained little data on the portfolio specialization of private equity companies. Based on the data available, I found that 16 per cent of the syndicates in the Neuer Markt sample, and 23 per cent of the syndicates in the Nouveau Marché sample are specialized in financing particular industries.

Regarding specialization in development stages, I focus on specialization in the early stage of firms' development. For this I created a dummy variable that is equal to one if each private equity company in the syndicate invests more than 50 per cent of its portfolio in the early stage of firms' development, and zero otherwise. There are ten syndicates in the Neuer Markt sample, and six syndicates in the Nouveau Marché sample in which each member has invested more than 50 per cent of its portfolio in the firms' early stage of development. These syndicates might be seen as being specialized in financing the early stage of firms' development. Thus, as compared to the total number of syndicates under consideration, there are only a few syndicates in which private equity companies have similar specialization patterns on industries and stages. This may indicate a bundling of complementary skills in private equity syndicates.

Recent empirical studies have analysed whether syndication of private equity investments takes place in order to reduce investment risks or to increase the resource pool that is important in the selection and in the investment stage. Studies that use data on European private equity companies are summarized in the following.[17]

Using a dataset of 62 firms, Lockett and Wright (2001) and Wright and Lockett (2003) have analysed syndication behaviour in the United Kingdom. Lockett and Wright (2001) have found evidence that the traditional finance perspective, that is, reduction of portfolio risk, is more important than increasing the resource pool available to the portfolio firms. The importance of syndication differs with the private equity companies' preference for investment size. The resource-based motive for syndication is more important for private equity companies whose investment size preference is comparatively low. Moreover, Lockett and Wright (2001) have found an increase in the resource pool due to syndication being more important for the investment stage than for the selection stage. Thus, having the opportunity to 'access specific skills in order to manage the investment' and 'to ask the advice of other venture capital firms' (Wright and Lockett 2001) is valuable to private equity companies. Wright and Lockett (2003) have reported that lead private equity companies in a syndicate hold larger equity stakes, are more likely to be represented on the board of directors, and are more active in monitoring and supporting the portfolio firms than the other private equity companies involved in the syndicates.

Using an initial public offering dataset on Neuer Markt firms, Lehmann and Boschker (2002) and Lehmann (2004) have analysed syndication behaviour in Germany. Lehman and Boschker (2002) have found that syndication is more likely to take place in firms operating in the biotechnology industry. Both the traditional finance motive and the resource pool motive can explain why syndication is higher in the biotechnology industry than in other industries. Financing biotechnology firms by several private equity companies might be particularly important because investment risks in this industry might be higher than in other industries, calling for diversification, and because asymmetric information between private equity companies and firms in this industry might be higher than in other industries, calling for an increase in the resource pool.

Lehman and Boschker (2002) have not found a significant effect of syndication on the probability of being de-listed from the Neuer Markt or the amount of capital raised. Lehmann (2004) has found that equity stakes held by private equity companies are higher in those firms that have been financed by a private equity syndicate, indicating a higher capital demand. Moreover, he has found that firms financed by a private equity syndicate realize higher employment growth than firms financed by a single private equity company. Thus, a private equity syndicate might add more value to portfolio firms than a single private equity company.

Using a dataset on private equity companies in six European countries, Manigart *et al.* (2004) have analysed syndication behaviour in Belgium, France, Germany, Sweden, the Netherlands and the United Kingdom. Their results show that syndication behaviour is very similar across European countries. For European private equity companies, risk sharing, portfolio diversification and access to larger deals are more important than increasing the resource pool necessary in the selection and investment stage. However, European private equity companies are not homogenous. Risk sharing is less important for large private equity companies, since they are able to realize a higher degree of diversification in their portfolios. Increasing the resource pool is a stronger motive for private equity companies specialized in the early stage than for those specialized in the later stages.

Summary

The investing phase of the venture capital cycle discussed in this chapter has many interesting facets. Countrywide data has shown that private equity is invested only in firms operating in particular industries and being in particular stages of development. There are several ways that private equity companies influence the risks and returns of private equity investments. At the individual deal level, private equity companies are actively involved in the portfolio firms by offering management support and monitoring. In addition, at the portfolio level, private equity companies specialize their portfolios in industries and sometimes in the early stage of development. Moreover, they build syndicates for financing portfolio firms. Syndication leads not only to a more diversified portfolio but also to a higher magnitude of experience in monitoring and supporting of portfolio firms.

5
Exiting

This chapter deals with the exiting behaviour of private equity companies. Private equity companies, especially those that are independent of their capital providers, aim at exiting from their participations in portfolio firms after some time. Exiting, which is the last stage in the venture capital cycle, plays an important role in this cycle, because a significant part of private equity companies' portfolio returns is realized when exiting from their participations.

The first part of this chapter describes exit channels used by private equity companies in European countries. The second part discusses developments in stock markets for fast-growing firms that influence developments in private equity industries. The third part focuses on what we know about the grandstanding and certification hypotheses. The last part discusses recent literature analysing the returns on private equity investments.

Exit channels

Private equity companies, especially those that are independent from their capital providers, exit from their participations after some time and repay the funds and returns to the capital providers. Several exit channels can be distinguished. First, private equity companies sell shares that they hold in portfolio firms *via* stock markets, either due to an initial public offering or a sale of already quoted equity. Second, they sell the shares that they hold in trade sales. Third, they sell shares to a portfolio firm's own managers or its founding entrepreneur. I will not focus on this channel in detail because data are not available. Fourth, in the case of a failure, they write off their participations in portfolio firms.

Preferences of US and European venture capital and private equity companies for the various exit channels differ. Schwienbacher (2002) has reported that 11 per cent of the European private equity companies consider the initial public offering as the most preferred exit channel compared to 29 per cent of the US venture capital companies. By contrast, 39 per cent of the European private equity companies have a strict preference for trade sales compared to 24 per cent of the US venture capital companies.

Table 5.1 informs on the relative importance of various exit channels that is, exiting volumes and exiting numbers for European countries based on the EVCA statistics. The data reported in this table show divestments as a percentage of total exits, averaged over the years 1991 to 2003. I did not use total exits from the EVCA statistics. Instead, I calculated total exits as the sum of exiting *via* stock markets, trade sales and write-offs because, in some years, a substantial amount of total exits reported in the EVCA statistics was not classified.

Compared to the fundraising and investment figures presented in Chapter 3 and 4, these data are likely to be of less quality in terms of representativeness because the number of private equity companies that reported their exits is very low (see, BVK 2000). Also, the number of exits as a percentage share of the number of private equity investments was as low as 21 per cent over all countries in 2000. This low percentage share was because relatively few private equity companies reported their exits and because European private equity industries boomed significantly at the end of the 1990s implying high investments that resulted in high exits only after some years.

Regarding the volume of exits, trade sales were the most important exit route during the observation period. They accounted for about 50 per cent of exits averaged over all the European countries considered. Sales *via* stock markets accounted only for 21 per cent of the total exit volume, on average. Write-offs accounted for less than 28 per cent of the total exit volumes. The percentage of write-offs understates the risk of venture capital investments because the data on exit volumes are based on private equity investments including buy-out activities and other forms of later-stage investments in established firms operating in traditional industries that are less risky than investments in young high-technology firms.

Regarding the number of exits, write-offs and trade sales were likewise relevant during the observation period. Write-offs accounted for 40 per cent averaged over all European countries considered, and trade sales accounted for about 41 per cent. Sales *via* stock markets accounted

Table 5.1 Exit channels

This table reports exits *via* various channels as a percentage of total exits, averaged over the years 1991 to 2003. Time trend is the coefficient of a time trend in a fixed effects model including year dummies, where the endogenous variable is the share of exits *via* a particular channel. *** (**,+) denotes significance at the 1 (5, 15) per cent level.

	Stock markets		Trade sales		Write-offs	
	Volume	Number	Volume	Number	Volume	Number
Austria	15.06	9.90	44.14	34.02	40.80	56.07
Belgium	19.75	14.42	51.77	45.00	28.48	40.58
Denmark	18.95	14.90	30.27	30.66	50.78	54.44
Finland	21.14	13.70	35.41	33.94	43.45	52.36
France	19.77	22.87	62.36	47.66	17.88	29.47
Germany	14.92	12.81	42.64	25.14	42.45	62.06
Greece	53.48	74.83	37.91	21.35	8.61	3.82
Ireland	4.52	4.38	72.24	59.63	23.24	35.99
Italy	11.85	7.94	73.62	70.35	14.52	21.72
Netherlands	17.60	14.36	58.02	46.82	24.38	38.82
Norway	34.11	28.36	34.67	24.79	31.22	46.85
Portugal	17.70	10.28	62.89	61.13	19.41	28.59
Spain	14.53	9.34	59.28	37.81	26.19	52.85
Sweden	27.83	20.90	50.46	43.34	21.71	35.76
Switzerland	30.06	35.56	32.25	27.67	37.69	36.77
United Kingdom	30.72	23.29	46.43	40.02	22.86	36.68
Total	21.47	18.76	50.16	41.40	28.38	39.84
Time Trend	1.54***	1.13***	–0.97+	–1.17**	–0.57	0.38

Source: EVCA (various issues), own calculations.

for only 19 per cent of the total exit number, on average. A comparison of the relative importance of exit channels measured by exit volumes and numbers indicates that successful private-equity-backed firms received higher amounts of investments, on average, than unsuccessful firms.

The relative importance of exit channels varied among European countries. In some countries, such as Norway, Sweden, Switzerland and the United Kingdom, exiting *via* stock markets accounted for about one-quarter of the exit volume.[18] In other countries, exiting *via* stock markets was not very important. In Ireland exiting *via* stock markets was as low as 5 per cent of the exit volume. Trade sales were very popular in Ireland and Italy, while they were unpopular in many other European countries. Write-offs varied from an average of 15 per cent in Italy, to more than 50 per cent in Denmark. These differences in write-offs among European countries stem partly from differences in the allocation of private equity across firms' development stages. According to Table 4.2, 12 per cent of private equity was invested in the early stage in Italy, while almost 26 per cent of private equity was invested in the early stage of firms' development in Denmark. In unreported fixed effects regressions, I tested whether there is a significant correlation between the allocation of private equity investments across development stages in previous years and the percentage shares of write-offs. I found a significantly positive correlation between the share of private equity invested in firms' early stage lagged twice and the percentage share of write-offs. Thus, countries having high early-stage investments may realize higher write-offs later on.

In order to give an impression of exiting over time, I ran fixed-effects regressions including a time trend where the endogenous variables were the shares of exiting *via* a particular exit channel to total exits. According to the coefficients of the time trend, which are reported in Table 5.1, exiting *via* stock markets increased significantly over time. This holds for the exiting volumes and the exiting numbers. According to the year dummies included in the regression, the relative importance of exiting *via* stock markets was systematically higher at the end of the 1990s than at the beginning of the 2000s. The relevance of trade sales decreased over time, while there was no time trend in the write-offs.

In order to describe the relevance of exiting *via* stock markets over time in more detail, I focus on three countries, namely Germany, the United Kingdom and France. Aggregated data on German exits show a substantial increase in exits *via* stock markets at the end of the 1990s. The exit volumes *via* stock markets including initial public offerings and sales of already quoted equity as a percentage of all exits reached a peak in 1999. Starting from about 5 per cent in 1997, exits *via* stock markets accounted for 24 per cent of all exits in 1998, and more than 29 per cent in 1999. In 2000, exits *via* stock markets started to decline. They accounted for 17 per cent in 2000, and only 7 per cent in 2002 (EVCA various issues). In 2003, however, exits *via* stock markets accounted again for 12 per cent. The decline in the relevance of exiting *via* stock markets was even stronger when looking at exits *via* initial public offerings only. Exits *via* initial public offerings accounted for almost 12 (9) per cent in 1999 (2000), while they accounted for less than 1 per cent in 2001 (BVK various issues).

In the United Kingdom, exits *via* stock markets, as a percentage of all exits, also peaked in 1999. In comparison to the German situation, however, exits *via* stock markets were also important in the middle of the 1990s (EVCA various issues). Exits *via* stock markets accounted for about 30 per cent in 1996, and 20 per cent in 1997. They accounted for 25 per cent in 1998 and reached more than 48 per cent of all exits in 1999. As with German exits *via* stock markets, British exits *via* stock markets dropped sharply after 1999. In 2000, they accounted for only 19 per cent of all exits. Contrary to the German situation, British exits *via* stock markets were again higher in 2002 and 2003. In these years, they accounted for 29 and 24 per cent, respectively. Similar to the development in Germany, British exits *via* initial public offerings were low in 2000 and 2001. In these years they accounted for less than 3 per cent of all exits.

In France, exits *via* stock markets reached a peak in 2000. Since the middle of the 1990s, French exits *via* stock markets, as a percentage of all exits, increased almost continuously. In 1995, exits *via* stock markets accounted for about 17 per cent of all exits, in 1996 they accounted for about 22 per cent, and in 1998 and 1999 they accounted for around 40 per cent (EVCA various issues). In 2000, exits *via* stock markets were almost 32 per cent. In 2001 and 2002, they accounted for almost 23 per cent. Thus, French exits *via* stock markets as a percentage of all exits developed differently than the British and German exits *via* stock markets. The latter two experienced a substantial decline between 1999 and 2000, while the former experienced a less strong decline between 2000 and 2001.

Developments in stock markets for fast-growing firms

Stock market segments for fast-growing firms are important for the developments in venture capital industries for at least four reasons.

First, in the United States, venture capital companies generate a main part of their returns by bringing firms to the public markets (Lerner 1994b). Second, by successfully exiting from venture-capital-backed firms *via* an initial public offering, venture capital companies build a reputation that they can use to raise funds from capital providers at more favourable conditions. Third, with initial public offerings of venture-capital-backed firms, venture capital companies can signal their experience to the market, and this can reduce transaction costs in the relationship between venture capital companies and entrepreneurs. Fourth, as Black and Gilson (1998) have argued, stock markets for fast-growing firms offer venture capital companies and entrepreneurs who want to start high-technology firms the opportunity to enter into an implicit contract over control. Because an initial public offering gives the entrepreneur the opportunity to reacquire control at least partly (since the entrepreneur can obtain a leading management position in the listed firm), the entrepreneur has lower incentives to engage in opportunistic behaviour (Bascha and Walz 2002a). Because of these four reasons, liquid stock markets for fast-growing firms are expected to increase venture capital investments.

Compared to the United States, European countries have difficulties in establishing special stock market segments for either small firms or high-technology firms. As soon as in the 1980s, several European countries launched second-tier markets that were designed for the raising of equity capital of small- and medium-sized firms (OECD 2002a). The main idea of these second-tier markets was to lower transaction costs for small- and medium-sized firms when raising external equity by introducing less restrictive listing requirements than those of the main markets. However, since these markets attracted insufficient liquidity they were closed or reorganized in the 1990s (OECD 2002a).

A second wave of establishing special stock market segments took place in the middle of the 1990s. Table 5.2 informs on selected characteristics of these stock market segments. In the United Kingdom, the *Alternative Investment Market* was established in 1995. The Alternative Investment Market is the world's leading small-cap growth market. In 2003 and 2004 this market accounted for 68 per cent of all initial public offerings in Western Europe. Currently, there are more than 790 issuers listed on the Alternative Investment Market, with a combined market capitalization of £21 billion. In France, the *Nouveau Marché* was established in 1996 and then closed in 2005. The Nouveau Marché was a market segment intended to meet the needs of fast-growing young firms seeking capital to finance expansion. In Germany,[19] the *Neuer*

Markt was established in 1997 and then closed in 2002. On a European-wide level, the EASDAQ was established in 1996, and was acquired by NASDAQ in 2001. Other European countries, such as Spain, Italy and Switzerland also established stock market segments for fast-growing firms.

In terms of the number of listed firms, their capitalization and amount of capital they raised in their initial public offerings, the NASDAQ is much larger than the European stock market segments. In terms of the number of listed firms, the Alternative Investment Market is larger than all other European markets. Before its closure, the Neuer Markt had a higher market capitalization than the Alternative Investment Market, but the daily transaction volume was higher in the Alternative Investment Market than in the Neuer Markt (De la Dehesa 2002).

Figure 5.1 graphs selected stock market indexes in Europe and the United States for the period March 10, 1997 to September 30, 2004. The indexes were rescaled to assume the value 100 on March 10, 1997. The figure shows that the indexes of high-technology firms increased substantially, while the indexes of blue chips did not. The indexes of high-technology firms show similar behaviour over time. However, the Nemax50 jumped substantially at the beginning of 1998, while the Alternative Investment Market and the Nouveau Marché indexes did not. In the second half of the 1990s, the NASDAQ Composite reached

Table 5.2 Stock markets for fast-growing firms in Europe and the United States

This table reports characteristics of stock markets for fast-growing firms. Listed firms and capitalization are for 2001, number of initial public offerings (IPOs) and amount of capital raised from the opening of the market (from 1990 for NASDAQ) through 2001. Capital raised and market capitalization are in millions of euros (millions of dollars for NASDAQ).

	Nouveau Marché	Neuer Markt	Milan Numtel	FTSE AIM	EASDAQ	NASDAQ
Year of opening	1996	1997	1999	1995	1996	1971
Listed firms	164	326	45	598	50	4,109
Number of IPOs	176	356	45	na	62	4,876
Market capitalization	15.011	49.933	14.801	na	8.000	2,899.000
Capital raised	2,966	21,611	4.042	na	2,300	293,364

Source: Adapted from Bottazzi and Da Rin (2002b).

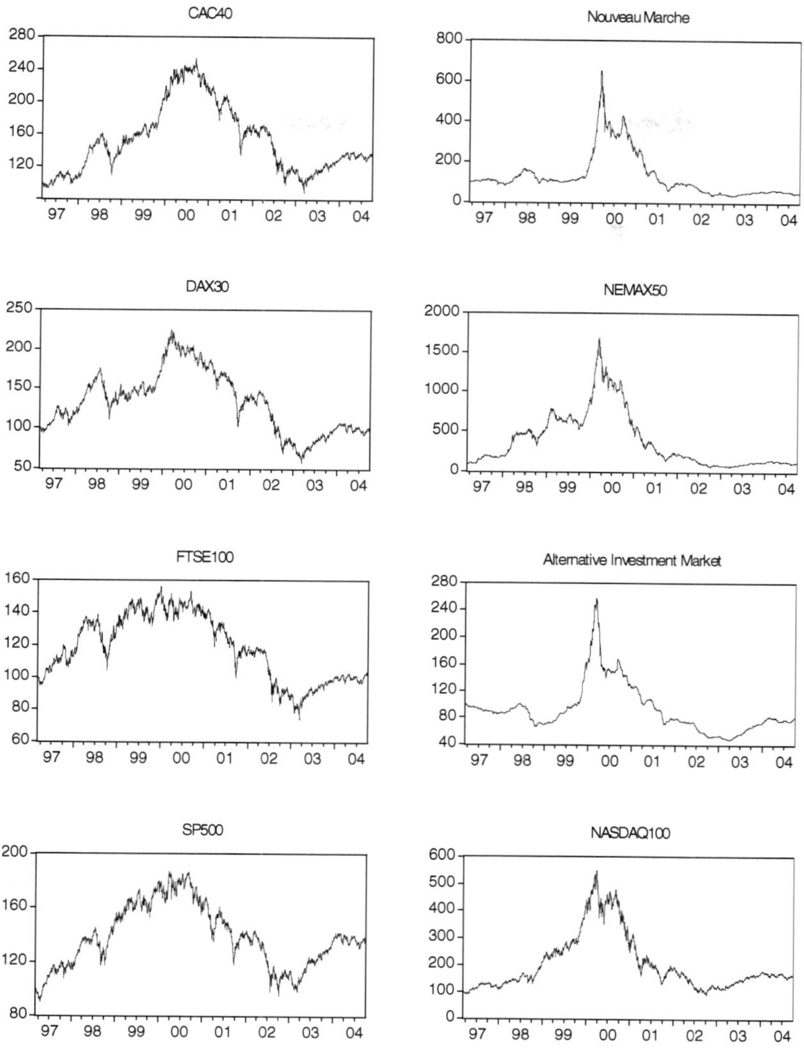

Figure 5.1 Developments of stock market indexes in Europe and the United States
This figure shows the developments in indexes for blue chip and for fast-growing firms. The CAC40 is a benchmark index based on a selection of 40 stocks listed on the Premier Marché and structured so as to reflect the full range of equities traded on Euronext Paris. The DAX30 is an index based on the 30 largest German firms officially listed on the Frankfurt Stock Exchange. The FTSE100 is an index based on a selection of 100 stocks listed on the Main Market of the London Stock Exchange. SP500 is the Standard and Poors 500 index. The Nemax50 is composed of the 50 largest high-technology firms listed on the Neuer Markt.
Source: Thomson Financial Datastream, own calculations.

a maximum of about 550 basis points, the Nemax50 a maximum of more than 1,600, the Nouveau Marché a maximum of about 650, and the Alternative Investment Market a maximum of only 250. These differences in basis points were driven by differences in the composition of the industries in the indexes. For example, the Nouveau Marché and the Neuer Markt included a higher percentage of firms operating in the information and communications industry than the Alternative Investment Market. Higher share prices were observed especially with firms operating in the information and communications industry.

Establishing stock market segments for fast-growing firms affected the exits of private equity companies. In Germany, for example, the number of exits *via* stock markets increased substantially after the foundation of the Neuer Markt (BVK various issues). In 1996, only 18 private-equity-backed firms went public, while in 2000, 67 private-equity-backed firms went public (BVK various issues). Out of these 67 firms, 60 firms went public on the Neuer Markt. Therefore, the Neuer Markt offered a liquid exit channel for private equity companies until 2000.

The bursting of the stock market bubble in 2000 affected European private equity industries negatively through several channels. First, most of private equity companies' portfolios became inflated in the course of the stock market bubble, and the bursting of the bubble led to large negative adjustments in the portfolio values. In Germany, for example, about 70 per cent of all exits were written-off in the second and third quarters of 2001.[20] In the first quarter of 2002 and in 2003, the respective number was only about 50 per cent. Second, the bursting of the stock market bubble affected the solvency of private equity companies listed on a stock exchange that experienced substantial losses in their share prices.

The climate on stock markets, the liquidity and existence of stock market segments for fast-growing firms not only affects exiting *via* public offerings but also exiting *via* trade sales. The reason for this is that the possibility of exiting *via* an initial public offering is likely to affect prices in a trade sale positively.

Hypotheses on certification and grandstanding

The establishment of stock markets for fast-growing firms in Europe has led to several datasets of initial public offerings that have been used to test the hypotheses on certification and grandstanding in private equity industries.

According to the hypothesis on certification, private equity companies are expected to certify the true value of their portfolio firms to other outside investors when bringing their portfolio firms to the public markets (Megginson and Weiss 1991). More specifically, the monitoring services of private equity companies are likely to be recognized by market participants that honour these services by demanding a lower risk premium when buying these shares for the first time (Barry *et al.* 1990). Therefore, private-equity-backed firms are expected to realize lower underpricing, which is defined as the spread between the opening price on the first trading day and the issue price, than comparable non-private-equity-backed firms when shares are offered for the first time to the public.

There are several studies analysing the certification role of venture capital companies using data from the United States. Barry *et al.* (1990), Megginson and Weiss (1991) and Lin and Smith (1998) have found that venture capital companies have a certification role. However, Francis and Hasan (2001) and Smart and Zutter (2000) have been able to corroborate this. In their analysis, underpricing is not significantly lower for venture-capital-backed than for non-venture-capital-backed firms. In addition, after controlling for the endogeneity in receiving venture capital finance, Lee and Wahal (2004) have found that venture-capital-backed firms realize a higher degree of underpricing in their initial public offerings than comparable non-venture-capital-backed firms.

Several studies have tested the hypothesis on certification using initial public offerings data from European stock markets. Kraus (2002), Franzke (2003), Stolpe (2003) and Tykvova and Walz (2004) have analysed whether private equity companies certify their portfolio firms' quality using data from the German Neuer Markt. Kraus (2002) has documented that private equity backing *per se* has no significant impact on underpricing. Franzke (2003) has controlled for private equity companies' experience and found evidence that high-ranked private equity companies increase underpricing of the firms' shares. However, Franzke (2003) has not controlled for different types that are active in the German private equity industry. Stolpe (2003), who has taken the heterogeneity in the German private equity industry into account, found that firms backed by older and thus more experienced private equity companies and by private equity companies specialized in high-technology fields realized higher underpricing, while firms backed by independent private equity companies realized lower underpricing. Tykvova and Walz (2004) have also controlled for the experience as well as for various types of private equity companies. According to their analysis, the type of a private equity company does not matter for the underpricing of the portfolio firms. In addition, their results support the findings of Franzke (2003) and Stolpe (2003); the higher the experience of a private equity company, the higher the degree of underpricing is. An open question is, however, what happens to these results if the endogeneity in the receipt of venture capital and private equity finance discussed in Lee and Wahal (2004) is taken into account.

The hypothesis on grandstanding deals with the behaviour of venture capital companies when exiting from their portfolio firms. More specifically, Gompers (1996) has argued that young venture capital companies take their portfolio firms to the public earlier (after shorter financing periods) than established venture capital companies do. The advantage of taking firms public earlier for young venture capital companies is that they can signal their experience in financing high-technology firms to the market so that they can raise new funds at more favourable conditions. Thus, one can expect that young venture capital companies raise new funds soon after taking firms public. What are the costs of such behaviour? Going public earlier can be associated with greater underpricing of the portfolio firms' shares because one can expect that the younger the firm is, the larger the ex-ante uncertainty between new and old shareholders. The larger the ex-ante uncertainty is, the higher the expected magnitude of underpricing might be. Using data from the United States, Gompers (1996) has found significant differences between young and established venture capital companies. According to his results, young venture capital companies bring their portfolio firms to the public markets earlier, and they have shorter financing periods than established venture capital companies.

Grandstanding has also been analysed for the British private equity industry. Barnes and McCarthy (2002) who have used a sample of 85 initial public offerings in the United Kingdom have found evidence that firms backed by young private equity companies are younger at the initial public offering than those backed by older and thus more established private equity companies. While young US venture capital companies raise new funds significantly earlier after the date of the initial public offering than their established counterparts (Gompers 1996), young British private equity companies do not differ from their established counterparts in this respect. In addition, in the sample by Gompers (1996), the shares of firms backed by young venture capital companies are more underpriced at their initial public offerings than the shares of firms backed by more established venture capital companies. By contrast, in the sample used by Barnes and McCarthy (2002), the firms backed by young private equity companies do not differ with respect to underpricing from their counterparts backed by more established private equity companies.

Returns

Calculating returns on venture capital and private equity investments is difficult because returns on portfolio firms are not available on a continuous basis (EVCA 2004b). Returns are available if the private equity companies exit from their portfolio firms, or if the portfolio firms receive additional funding. This gives rise to severe concerns about biases in measuring returns. More specifically, the general partners in a limited partnership may correct the value of an investment only after severe changes have taken place, leading to a so-called *stale pricing bias*. The returns on private equity investments are not easily comparable to other asset classes because of the illiquidity of investments in private equity funds.

The returns on private equity investments can be analysed for various aggregation levels with various indicators. With respect to the aggregation level, the returns on private equity investments can be based either on the level of the portfolio firms, or on the level of the private equity funds, or they can be based on the level of a whole country or region. With respect to the indicators used, the most common one is the internal rate of return (IRR), which does not offer, however, information on the risk-return profile of private equity investments or funds.[21] Estimations of a risk-return profile of private equity investments are based on modern portfolio theory.

Venture Economics has prepared an annual *Pan-European Investment Benchmark Study* on European countries using the IRR technique and funds data. This study provides a comparison of the performance of European private equity with other asset classes on the basis of equivalent net IRR. *Net* means that the often substantial management fees for private equity companies have already been deducted. To calculate equivalent IRRs, the same pattern of private equity investments and exiting over time as in the private equity dataset have been utilized to construct a portfolio of an alternative asset class.

According to the Investment Benchmark Study of 2001 (EVCA 2002a) the net cumulative annualized IRR of all European private equity funds in the sample outperformed alternative asset classes.

European private equity funds had a net cumulative annualized IRR of more than 12 per cent. By contrast, the equivalent IRRs of Morgan Stanley Capital International (MSCI) Equity was only 8.9 per cent, the equivalent IRR of JP Morgan Bond was lower at 7.0 per cent, and the equivalent IRR of HSBC Small Cap was as low as −1.2 per cent. MSCI Equity contains larger and HSBC Small Cap contains smaller firms.

Moreover, the net cumulative annualized IRR of funds invested in the early stage of firms' development outperformed alternative asset classes. However, while the net cumulative annualized IRR of funds invested in the early stage was 8.9 per cent, the net cumulative annualized IRR of funds invested in venture capital was 12 per cent, and the net cumulative annualized IRR of funds invested in management buy-outs was 14.8 per cent. Similar results are documented in EVCA (2004b), a study that is based on the cashflow data of 201 European private equity funds. According to this study, the IRR of management buy-out funds was as high as 13.4 per cent, compared to 10.6 per cent of venture capital funds.

While the Investment Benchmark Study of 2001 showed that the returns of almost all private equity subgroups outperformed the returns of other asset classes, the Investment Benchmark Study of 2000 showed a less clear picture (EVCA 2001a). In particular, in 2000, several subgroups of private equity funds had a lower net cumulative annualized IRR than MSCI Equity, or HSBC Small Cap. For example, the net cumulative annualized IRR of funds invested in the early stage and all venture capital had a lower return than MSCI Equity.

Comparing the returns on private equity reported for 2000 and 2001 shows that the return on private equity decreased for many groups of private equity. While the Investment Benchmark Study of 2000 reported an IRR on all private equity of 15.6 per cent, the Investment Benchmark Study of 2001 reported an IRR on all private equity of only 12.7 per cent, which is comparatively high given the fall in value on European stock markets.

Recent empirical literature has analysed determinants of returns on private equity investments. Four groups of factors, which I will discuss in more detail below, are likely to affect returns on private equity investments. First, general market developments such as inflows of new funds may affect returns on private equity investments. Second, certain characteristics of private equity companies' portfolios such as specializations in particular stages of firms' development may affect returns on private equity companies. Third, certain characteristics of private equity companies such as skills and the intensity of monitoring services may affect returns on private equity investments. Fourth, certain investment characteristics of portfolio firms such as age, industry, and the management skills of their founders, as well as the contractual design between the private equity company and the portfolio firm, may affect the returns on private equity investments.

Regarding general market developments, Gompers and Lerner (2000) have argued that capital inflows to the venture capital industry affect returns if the magnitude of the change in capital inflows exceeds the magnitude of the change in the number of promising investment opportunities. Such a mismatch between capital inflows and venture capital demand can reduce returns, because of the characteristics that are specific to the venture capital asset class. This *money chasing deals* phenomenon implies a negative correlation between capital inflows and returns on venture capital investments.

Using a dataset of 200 mature European private equity funds, Diller and Kaserer (2005) have tested whether capital inflows and returns on private equity funds are negatively related. Diller and Kaserer (2005) have documented that the money chasing deals phenomenon helps in explaining a large part of the variation in returns on private equity investments. The effects are even stronger for venture capital funds than for management buy-out funds.

Ljungqvist and Richardson (2003) have also analysed market conditions for the performance of private equity investments. Based on 73 mature private equity funds raised between 1981 and 1993, Ljungqvist and Richardson (2003) have calculated and analysed multiples on investments, defined as abs (cash inflows/invested capital). Fourteen per cent of the portfolio firms under consideration generated capital loses, 55 per cent generated a multiple of zero, almost 12 per cent generated multiples between one and two, 6.3 per cent generated multiples between two and three, and 12.9 per cent generated multiples larger than three. Multiples of zero were much more common for venture capital funds (77.3 per cent) than for private equity funds (37.8 per cent). Ljungqvist and Richardson (2003) have converted multiples of investments into annualized returns in order to take the time structure of investments and exiting into account. They have tested whether the annualized returns depend systematically on changes in the demand and supply conditions in private equity industries. Improvements in investment opportunities have a positive effect on the annualized returns. By contrast, an increase in competition for deal flows reduces annualized returns.

Regarding the characteristics of private equity companies' portfolios, Hege *et al.* (2003), who have used data from the United States and Europe, have found that their performance measures depend on the investment allocation in private equity companies' portfolios. More specifically, their first performance measure, the share of successful exits that occurred *via* initial public offerings and trade sales, decreases with the percentage of private equity companies' portfolios invested in the early stage of firms' development. In addition, their second performance measure, the natural logarithm of excess returns, is negatively related to the amount invested in the early stage, and positively related to the ratio of the amount invested in the early stage relative to the discounted total investments. In a related study, Manigart *et al.* (2002) have found evidence that private equity companies specialized in financing the early stage of firms' development demand significantly higher returns than private equity companies financing later stages of firms' development.

Regarding characteristics of private equity companies, Cumming and Walz (2004) have found that private equity companies' monitoring services have a significantly positive impact on the IRR using an international sample of private equity funds. In addition, Cumming and Walz (2004) have analysed unrealized IRRs that private equity companies report to their capital providers. In this part of their analysis, they have focused on the trade-off faced by private equity companies between facilitating fundraising and hurting their reputation by reporting overestimated IRRs to their capital providers. They have found systematic differences between realized and unrealized IRRs; the median of the unrealized IRRs is zero per cent, while the median of the realized IRRs is about 17 per cent. Proxies for information asymmetries between private equity companies, on the one hand, and capital providers, on the other hand, help in explaining the differences in realized and unrealized IRRs.

Returns on private equity investments are also likely to depend on the type of the private equity company. According to the study by Manigart *et al.* (2002), independent private equity companies located in the United States, the United Kingdom, the Netherlands, France and Belgium demand significantly higher returns than their dependent counterparts for investments in firms' early and expansion stages. These higher return demands are correlated with a higher intensity of private equity companies' monitoring and management support services (Manigart *et al.* 2002). According to the study by Bascha and Walz (2002b), government-based private equity companies have significantly lower return demands than other private equity companies in Germany. In their analysis, which is based on a questionnaire approach, return demands can take three values; they can either be below, above, or at the industry average. Neither the age of the private equity company nor the number of firms in private equity companies' portfolios helps in explaining return demands.

Regarding investment characteristics, Hege *et al.* (2003) have found that the natural logarithm of excess returns is positively related to the total duration of the investment measured as the time between the first and the last round of investment in a portfolio firm. Most interestingly, for their US sample, the natural logarithm of excess returns turns out to be negatively related to the total duration, while for their European sample it turns out to be positively related. Therefore, Hege *et al.* (2003) have argued that European private equity companies seem to have lesser screening capacities than their US counterparts. Using an international sample of private equity funds, Cumming and Walz (2004) have found that the characteristics of the portfolio firms, the investment deals, and a legality index help in explaining more than 45 per cent of the variation in their data on IRRs. The use of incentive-increasing financial instruments such as convertible securities and the legality index of the countries have a significantly positive impact on the IRR.

Summary

This chapter has discussed the exiting of private equity companies from their participations in portfolio firms. Private equity companies use either a sale *via* stock markets, a trade sale, or they write off the participations they held in the portfolio firms. For European countries, trade sales are the most relevant exit channel in terms of the divestment volume; sales *via* stock markets play a relevant role only in particular countries, such as the United Kingdom, or in particular years, such as the years at the end of the 1990s, which were characterized by higher stock prices. The recent empirical literature indicates that, when exiting from their participations, European private equity companies do not certify the true value of their portfolio firms to other outside investors. Exiting plays a special role, since in this stage of the venture capital cycle, private equity companies realize a significant part of their returns. Returns on private equity investments do not only depend on general market trends determining selling conditions for portfolio firms but also on certain characteristics of private equity companies, such as the type and investment strategies discussed in Chapters 3 and 4.

6
Cross-Country Variations in Investments

This chapter deals with cross-country variations in venture capital and private equity investments. It differs from the previous chapters in two main regards. First, it focuses exclusively on the industry features in Europe's private equity industries, while previous chapters have likewise focused on the microeconomics of venture capital finance and, to a lesser extent, on its industry features. Second, the aim of this chapter is not mainly to summarize the results of recent research but to analyse empirically the determinants of cross-country variations in investments. This analysis draws substantially from the insights of the previous chapters.

The first part of this chapter introduces the empirical model. The second part describes the exogenous variables of the empirical model. The third and fourth part presents estimation results for percentage changes in various types of private equity investments such as early-stage investments, early- and expansion-stage investments, and total private equity investments.

Empirical model

The empirical model considers a lagged endogenous variable, a set of determinants that I will discuss below, and fixed effects (country-specific effects):

$$PE_{it} = PE_{it-1}\,\delta + X_{it}\,\beta + C_i + \varepsilon_{it} \qquad (6.1)$$

where PE_{it} denotes the growth in private equity investments in country i in year t, X_{it} denotes the row vector of exogenous variables, C_i denotes the country-specific effects, e_{it} is the error term.

Estimating a dynamic model and using dynamic panel data techniques seems sensible because of the dynamic processes likely taking place in venture capital and private equity industries. In particular, venture capital and private equity companies have to accumulate experience and to build reputation. Experience is needed to successfully select, monitor, support and, thus, to add value to young high-technology firms. Venture capital companies accumulate experience by being involved in the management of young high-technology firms. Reputation, that is, a track record of successfully financing young high-technology firms, is needed in order to raise capital from capital providers at favourable conditions. Capital providers have a priori little information about the profitability of private equity investments and the experience of private equity companies in financing high-technology firms. By estimating a dynamic model, the effects of experience accumulation and reputation building can be captured.

The empirical model in equation (6.1) differs from existing studies with respect to the calculation of the endogenous variable. I used the annual percentage changes in private equity investments. Using annual percentage changes allow European countries of different sizes to be compared. Recent literature has used other measures that also control for the different sizes of the countries and states. For their study on venture capital investments in US states, Gompers and Lerner (1999b) have used venture capital investments relative to population. For their studies on private equity industries in European countries, Da Rin *et al.* (2004) have used early-stage investments as a percentage of total private equity investments, Romain and van Pottelsberghe (2004) have used private equity investments relative to GDP and Schertler (2005b) has used first differences of private equity investments relative to GDP.

At the centre of the scaling procedure is not only the intention to control for the different sizes of European countries but also to construct a stationary time series, since the degree of integration affects the empirical specification that can be used. Employing the panel unit root tests developed by Levin *et al.* (2002), which assumes identical coefficients of the lagged endogenous variable across countries, and the test developed by Im *et al.* (2003), which allows heterogeneous coefficients of the lagged endogenous variables across countries, Schertler (2005b) has shown that the hypothesis of non-stationarity for the volume of various types of private equity investments relative to GDP or the number of various types of private equity investments relative to the population cannot be rejected. Therefore, levels of private equity investments relative to GDP are not stationary, while first differences of investments relative to GDP and the percentage changes in investments are stationary.

I followed Gompers and Lerner (1999b) and used the number of investments in addition to the volume of investments. Using the number of investments is of particular interest, since high volumes of investments, which may indicate a well-developed private equity industry, can be the result of few large investments, so that only few firms are private-equity-backed. Thus, the relevance of the private equity industry on a countrywide basis can be overestimated when using solely investment volumes.

Country-specific effects have to be removed from equation (6.1) because they are likely to be correlated with the lagged endogenous variable. They can be removed by calculating first differences. Anderson and Hsiao (1982) were the first to propose this approach. I estimated equation (6.1) by using the generalized method of moments (GMM) estimator proposed by Blundell and Bond (1998) and a finite sample correction proposed by Windmeijer (2005). This also allows coefficients of time-invariant variables such as countries' legal tradition to be estimated. Estimation results are unbiased if appropriate instruments for the lagged endogenous variable are used and if there is no second-order autocorrelation. Therefore, I performed tests on serial correlation, using a test of the second-order residual correlation coefficient, and I performed a test of over-identifying restrictions to check the validity of my instruments (Blundell and Bond 1998).

Description of variables

In Chapters 3 to 5, I have already discussed several determinants that are likely to affect the fundraising, investing and exiting behaviours of private equity companies. In this chapter, I summarize and discuss only those determinants that are available for an empirical analysis based on a cross-country time-series dataset. The endogenous and exogenous variables used in the empirical analysis are described in detail in Table A3.

The determinants discussed in the following are: the style of financial intermediation and financial markets, such as pension funds and stock markets for fast-growing firms, the role of European governments in venture capital industries, capital gains taxes, conditions for entrepreneurships, for example, the countries' human capital endowments and macroeconomic conditions. Table 6.1 gives the mean values of the exogenous variables used in the empirical analysis.

Table 6.1 Description of the variables used

This table reports the exogenous variables used in Tables 6.2 and 6.3, averaged here over the years 1991 to 2001. For data definitions see Table A3.

	Growth rate of new funds	Stock market returns	Stock market return volatility	Growth rate of patents	Labour index	Firm creation index	Entrepreneurship index	Short-term interest rate	Growth rate of GDP
Austria	47.12	–0.017	1.132	5.42	2.20	5.43	11.70	5.24	3.43
Belgium	26.39	–0.017	1.132	7.45	2.37	6.51	6.13	5.38	3.56
Denmark	23.07	–0.017	1.132	8.83	1.45	5.64	11.92	6.17	4.46
Finland	28.30	–0.017	1.132	10.37	2.08	6.75	12.16	6.10	6.83
France	14.91	–0.009	1.183	3.41	2.92	5.42	10.25	5.77	2.82
Germany	14.70	0.033	1.209	5.69	2.69	6.23	11.92	5.24	2.78
Greece	23.20	–0.017	1.132	9.00	3.60	7.48	11.20	14.10	15.30
Ireland	22.17	–0.017	1.132	11.56	0.90	7.64	12.23	6.77	12.19
Italy	22.67	–0.017	1.132	5.08	3.52	7.26	12.29	7.96	7.71
Netherlands	18.77	–0.017	1.132	8.26	2.21	7.15	12.29	5.12	4.80
Norway	16.90	–0.017	1.132	8.94	2.71	6.73	9.30	6.90	7.18
Portugal	16.02	–0.017	1.132	14.63	3.81	6.73	8.80	8.75	8.95
Spain	16.22	–0.060	0.550	10.93	3.26	5.93	10.38	7.66	9.49
Sweden	23.23	–0.017	1.132	7.08	2.55	6.58	12.48	6.74	4.02
Switzerland	15.91	–0.017	1.132	4.33	1.00	6.67	12.41	3.71	2.10
United Kingdom	19.31	–0.004	0.469	3.66	0.50	7.39	10.38	6.91	5.43

Source: see Table A3.

Financial intermediation and financial markets

The style of financial intermediation and financial markets may explain cross-country variations in private equity investments. I distinguish between four potential determinants that are related to the style of financial intermediation and financial markets that I will discuss in more detail below. First, investments in firms' early stage of development may depend on the supply conditions in venture capital and private equity industries. Second, pension funds may be important capital providers that may also determine the characteristics of firms in which venture capital and private equity is invested. Third, the financial architecture reflected by the assets of financial intermediaries relative to stock market capitalization may be a potential determinant of cross-country variations in private equity investments, since it may capture the financing structure of firms and the existence of capital providers. Fourth, developments in stock market segments for fast-growing firms may be important for developments in venture capital and private equity industries because exiting *via* initial public offerings might be important for the overall success and returns on private equity investments.

The supply conditions in venture capital and private equity industries are likely to affect the investments in firms' early stage of development. A boost in new funds raised for private equity investments may lead to investments of larger size and not to a larger number of investments (Gompers 1998, Wasserman 2003). Because firms in the early stage of development cannot absorb as much capital as firms in the expansion stage (Wasserman 2003), one can expect a negative link between early-stage investments and growth in new funds. In the empirical analysis, I capture supply conditions in the private equity industries by changes in the growth of new funds raised for private equity investments. According to Table 6.1, some European countries have been characterized by high growth rates in new funds. For example, averaged over the years 1991 to 2001, Austria realized a growth rate in new funds of 47 per cent. By contrast, France, and Germany realized a growth rate in new funds of about only 15 per cent.

Pension funds are likely to have a substantial impact on the developments in private equity industries. In the United States, changes in the regulation of investment activities of pension funds have had a significant effect on the development of the venture capital industry (Gompers and Lerner 1999b, Lerner 2002b). In particular, in 1979, the revision of the Employee Retirement Income Security Act (ERISA) 'Prudent Man' Rule allowed US pension funds higher-risk investments.

But pension funds may not only be important for supplying substantial amounts of funds provided for private equity investments. Their investment activity may also be important for developing new corporate governance structures in venture capital and private equity companies. Pension funds invest in independent private equity companies that have a higher propensity to invest in firms' early stages than in private equity companies that are dependent on banks. Independent private equity companies may have stronger incentives to develop control mechanisms to mitigate moral hazard and adverse selection problems when financing young high-technology firms than their dependent counterparts that obtain funds from private or savings banks.

The impact of pension funds on the private equity industry in a cross-country sample is determined by two characteristics of the pension funds industry. First, the impact of pension funds on private equity investments depends on the pension funds' assets under management in the country. Second, the impact of pension funds on private equity investments depends on the percentage share of the pension funds' portfolio that is allowed to be invested into high-risk asset classes. Both, the assets under management of pension funds and the percentage share of the assets allowed to be invested into high-risk asset classes vary substantially between European countries as I have shown in Chapter 3. Therefore, in the empirical analysis, I capture the activity of pension funds by including new funds provided by pension funds for private equity investments relative to the total of new funds provided for private equity investments. This variable reflects both the size of pension funds' assets under management and the regulations regarding the portfolio share that is allowed to be invested into high-risk asset classes. Moreover, this variable also reflects whether venture capital and private equity investments are likely to be a promising investment alternative in a particular country.

Differences in venture capital and private equity activity may be the result of differences in the financial architecture of the economies, since the financial architecture affects the capital allocation (Levine and Zervos 1998, Beck and Levine 2002). In many European countries, banks are the major players, while, in the United States, shareholders play an important role. Banks seem to have many disadvantages with respect to financing young high-technology firms especially because the control mechanisms of banks do not work well in the case of these firms. High-technology firms that invest a large part of their capital into research and development activities cannot offer collateral. Thus, collateral is not at the bank's disposal as a selection and monitoring mechanism. Additionally, bank managers are less likely to have enough experience to select the most promising high-technology firms. I capture the financial architecture by using bank assets relative to the number of firms listed on stock markets. I assume that a higher ratio of bank assets to stock markets has a negative impact on venture capital and private equity investments.

Developments in stock market segments for fast-growing firms are of particular relevance for developments in private equity investments for the reasons I have discussed in Chapter 5. In order to capture developments in stock market segments for fast-growing firms, I created a variable of annual stock market returns calculated from daily return indexes of Europe's stock markets for fast-growing firms (see also Schertler 2005b). For Germany I used the share index of the Neuer Markt founded in 1997, for France I used the share index of the Nouveau Marché founded in 1996, for Spain I used the share index of the Nuevo Mercado founded in 2000, and for the United Kingdom I used the share index of the Alternative Investment Market founded in 1995. For all other countries, I used the share index of the EASDAQ (European Association of Securities Dealers Automated Quotation) founded in 1996. From the daily stock market indexes, I calculated daily continuous returns. To get annual data, I calculated averages over daily returns. For the years before stock markets for fast-growing firms were set up, I set the average daily returns equal to zero. According to Table 6.1, European stock markets for fast-growing firms realized negative stock market returns during the years 1991 to 2001 which were driven by the sharp drop in share prices in 2000 and 2001. An exception concerning negative stock market returns was the German Neuer Markt.

A potential determinant for cross-country variations in private equity investments may not only be the returns on stock markets for fast-growing firms but also the volatility of these stock market returns. High volatility of stock market returns is often associated with increasing stock market returns. Since venture capital companies are likely to care about the time in which they take their portfolio firms to the public equity markets (Lerner 1994b), the volatility of stock market returns is expected to have a positive impact on venture capital and private equity investments. Therefore, I calculated the stock market return volatility from daily stock market returns based on indexes of fast-growing firms. According to the average values presented in Table 6.1, stock market return volatility was highest in the German Neuer

Markt, followed by the French Nouveau Marché and the EASDAQ. Stock market return volatility was very low in the British Alternative Investment Market.

European governments

European governments have taken an active role in establishing venture capital industries for high-technology firms, as I have already discussed in Chapter 3. European government support programmes are likely to have a positive and significant impact on the level of early-stage investments. This, however, does not mean that government support programmes are efficient. More specifically, that government support programmes likely have a positive and significant impact on early-stage investments informs only on these support programmes' impact on the volume of investments but not on whether they lead to a reduction in a probably existing capital shortage for young high-technology firms.

I take the role of European governments into account by including the share of new funds provided by European governments divided by total new funds. This measure of the relevance of governments has clear interpretation limits. This measure does not inform on the total impact of government-provided funds on private equity investments because it does not include the funds provided by local governments. In addition, this measure does not provide information on the impact of the government support programmes because it does not include guaranteed loans to non-government-based private equity companies. The advantage of this measure is that it is available for many European countries over a long time period.

Tax and legal environment

Capital gains taxes are likely to have a significant impact on the capital providers' portfolio decisions, since they can favour particular forms of investments. For example, capital providers have lower incentives to invest in venture capital funds and higher incentives to invest in bonds when losses made with venture capital investments are not tax deductible. I include the capital gains taxes emphasized, for example, by Gompers and Lerner (1999b) and Poterba (1989). As I have discussed in Chapter 3, the capital gains tax rate can differ between individuals within countries, since in some countries the income tax rate is partly used to tax capital gains. In the following empirical analysis, I ignore this fact and include the capital gains tax rate published in the Corporate Tax Guide.

The legal environment may affect developments in private equity industries in various ways. Better anti-director rights are expected to have a positive effect on returns on equity investments and, thus, on private equity investments, and a negative effect on the risks of these investments, since they protect shareholders. Accounting standards are expected to also have a positive effect on private equity investments, since they reduce transaction costs arising when investors gather information. Better accounting standards imply an easier and cheaper access to firm-specific information. Moreover, legal traditions may influence developments in private equity industries.

Entrepreneurship conditions

Entrepreneurship conditions may determine the demand for venture capital and private equity finance. I have discussed some of these conditions in Chapter 2. In the following, I therefore focus only on those conditions of entrepreneurship which can be used in a cross-country panel analysis. More specifically, I argue that the demand for venture capital finance depends on human capital, on labour market regulations and on the conditions of creating new firms.

As I have argued in Schertler (2005b), countries with a high amount of human capital are likely to have higher volumes of venture capital investments because more innovative ideas are developed for businesses that require venture capital finance for their start-up. The reason for this is that founders of high-technology start-ups must be highly skilled, and because they need employees who are also highly skilled. Finance provided by family members and friends cannot fulfill high capital needs of high-technology start-ups. Banks can also not fulfill the high capital needs because start-ups in high-technology industries are not likely to have enough collateral necessary to receive bank credits, partly because they often invest in intangible assets. Thus, the solution to this financing problem is to demand capital combined with high-quality monitoring provided by experienced venture capital companies. In the empirical analysis, I capture the countries' human capital by using the growth rate in the number of patent applications to the European patent office (for alternative measures of human capital, see Schertler 2005b). According to the average growth rates presented in Table 6.1, some countries, such as Finland, Portugal, Spain and Ireland had high growth rates in patenting during the observation period, while other countries, such as France and Switzerland had only moderate growth rates. I used the lag of the growth rate of patent applications in the empirical analysis because my measure of human capital endowments can be the result of venture capital finance; patents can be the result of such finance, since venture-capital-backed firms take out significantly more patents than other comparable firms (Kortum and Lerner 2000).

Entrepreneurship is likely to depend on the design of labour markets. Strong labour market institutions may lead to a substitution effect between capital and labour, resulting in higher capital-labour ratios (Layard *et al.* 1991, Jeng and Wells 2000). However, hold-up problems between firms and labour market institutions such as labour unions may reduce investment incentives (Grout 1984). As an approximation of labour market rigidities, I use an indicator of the strictness of protection against dismissals of regular and temporary employment published by the OECD.

In order to capture conditions for creating new firms, I use a firm creation index and an entrepreneurship index. A high value of the firm creation index indicates that the creation of firms is supported by legislation. France and Austria have comparatively low values on the firm creation index, while Greece, Ireland, Italy and the United Kingdom have high values. A high value on the entrepreneur index indicates that entrepreneurship is widespread in the economy.

Macroeconomic conditions

The role of macroeconomic conditions for financial intermediation has been analysed extensively in the literature on bank lending behaviour. In particular, this literature analyses the implications of monetary policy and business cycles on bank lending. Regarding monetary policy, many studies have analysed the channels through which monetary policy affects bank lending. Kashyap and Stein (2000), who have analysed the reaction of bank lending to changes in monetary policies, have found evidence that bank lending is reduced after a monetary shock. Regarding business cycles, Goldberg (2002, 2005) and Goldberg *et al.* (2002) have analysed how lending of US banks responds to domestic and foreign business cycles. They have found that cyclical developments explain bank lending. However, the impact of cyclical developments is not stable over time. In order to capture macroeconomic conditions that are also likely to affect private equity investments, I include the short-term interest rate and the annual percentage change in GDP in the empirical analysis. According to Table 6.1, there is heterogeneity regarding the short-term interest rates and the growth rate of GDP for European countries.

Estimation results

Table 6.2 shows the estimation results of my baseline regressions for percentage changes in early-stage investments, early- and expansion-stage investments, and private equity investments. In these baseline regressions I did not include those variables related to the entrepreneurial environment that I discuss as a robustness check below.

The lagged endogenous variables have negative coefficients, albeit they are not always significant. More specifically, the lagged endogenous variable is insignificant in the number of early- and expansion-stage investments equation, and in the volume of private equity investments equation. As indicated by the p-values of AR2, the error terms lack second-order correlation, which is necessary for GMM estimators to be consistent. The p-values of the Hansen tests indicate that the null hypothesis cannot be rejected. Under the null hypothesis, the model is correctly specified and the instruments are uncorrelated with the error term. Thus, both tests indicate that the regressions give consistent parameter estimations.

Which determinants help in explaining cross-country variations in private capital investments? Regarding the variables related to the style of financial intermediation and financial markets, I found mixed evidence. Changes in supply conditions in private equity industries captured by the percentage change in new funds do not help in explaining the percentage change in either early-stage investments, or early- and expansion-stage investments or private equity investments. This is in line with earlier evidence presented in Schertler (2005b), who has also not reported a significant effect of growth in new funds on early-stage investments.

New funds provided by pension funds affect the percentage changes of all the endogenous variables positively, albeit they are only significant in the case of the volume of private equity investments. Recent literature has analysed the role of pension funds by including the wealth of pension funds into the regression analysis instead of the share of new funds provided by pension funds. Jeng and Wells (2000) have found evidence that the wealth of private pension funds is a significant determinant of private equity fundraising over time but not across countries. Schertler (2004) has not found a significant relationship between pension funds' assets under management and private equity investments. As I have mentioned before, pension funds' assets are a poor measure of the relevance of pension funds for venture capital industries on a country level because they are allowed to invest different shares of their assets in unquoted firms.

Table 6.2 Determinants of venture capital and private equity investments
This table reports regression results for the determinants of venture capital and private equity investments. Endogenous variables are annual percentage changes. GMM estimations with absolute Windmeijer's (2005) corrected t-statistics are reported. SVC denotes investments in the early stage. DVC denotes investments in the firms' early and expansion stages. PE denotes private equity investments. N denotes the number of investments used instead of the volume. (1) denotes the first lag. *** (**, *) denotes significance at the 1 (5, 10) per cent level.

	(1) SVC	(2) SVCN	(3) DVC	(4) DVCN	(5) PE	(6) PEN
Endogenous variable (1)	–0.202**	–0.147*	–0.206*	–0.126	–0.038	–0.150**
	(2.55)	(1.86)	(1.87)	(1.66)	(0.43)	(2.22)
Growth rate of new funds (1)	–0.06	–0.036	–0.047	–0.034	–0.08	–0.045
	(0.7)	(0.5)	(1.51)	(1.13)	(1.24)	(1.33)
New funds by pension funds (1)	0.572	0.761	0.652	0.026	1.193*	0.202
	(0.87)	(1.44)	(0.62)	(0.07)	(1.81)	(0.63)
Bank assets to listed firms	0	0	0	0	0	0
	(0.22)	(1.08)	(0.64)	(0.38)	(0.55)	(0.48)
Stock market returns	1.264***	1.095***	0.758***	0.713***	0.940***	0.703***
	(3.82)	(4.42)	(3.18)	(3.21)	(5.47)	(3.35)
Stock market return volatility	0.291***	0.190***	0.154***	0.107**	0.105**	0.096***
	(4.11)	(3.76)	(3.15)	(2.94)	(2.85)	(3.38)
New funds by governments	0.007	0.013*	0.001	0.001	0.004	0.003
	(1.05)	(1.84)	(0.19)	(0.2)	(1.66)	(1.02)
Capital gains tax rate	–0.01	–0.011**	0.003	0.003	0.001	0.003
	(1.72)	(2.36)	(0.99)	(1.25)	(0.42)	(1.14)
Law tradition	–0.168	–0.242	–0.142	–0.128	–0.250*	–0.181
	(0.4)	(0.78)	(0.8)	(0.92)	(2.09)	(1.6)
Growth rate of patents (1)	1.711***	1.109***	–0.289	–0.03	–0.573	–0.16
	(3.28)	(4.8)	(0.56)	(0.12)	(1.2)	(0.62)
Labour index	–0.026	–0.021	0.005	–0.052	0.034	–0.051
	(0.12)	(0.16)	(0.05)	(0.68)	(0.58)	(0.92)
Short-term interest rate	–0.025	–0.034	–0.024	–0.024	–0.032	–0.021
	(0.49)	(1.34)	(0.8)	(1.22)	(1.57)	(1.35)
Growth rate of GDP	1.443	2.288	0.664	0.786	0.965	0.828*
	(0.91)	(1.62)	(0.79)	(1.32)	(1.02)	(2.11)
Number of observations	147	147	150	150	150	150
Number of countries	16	16	16	16	16	16
F-test	11.6***	168.6***	6.1***	20.3***	27.0***	31.5***
Hansen test (p-value)	0.16	0.595	0.337	0.342	0.6	0.362
AR1 (p-value)	0.015	0.004	0.01	0.008	0.007	0.013
AR2 (p-value)	0.647	0.823	0.475	0.198	0.631	0.178

Source: see Table A3.

Recent literature has also analysed whether the provision of more funds provided by pension funds lead to more early-stage investments. So far, the literature is not conclusive on this point. Using qualitative micro-data on private equity companies, Mayer *et al.* (2005) have documented that private equity companies receiving capital from pension funds are less likely to invest in firms at an early stage of development. By contrast, using the EVCA statistics, Schertler (2005b) has found that new funds provided by pension funds have a positive and significant impact on the number of early-stage investments but not on early- and expansion-stage investments. Moreover, Schertler (2005a) has documented that new funds provided by pension funds, as compared to corporate investors, are more often used in financing early-stage deals than later-stage deals. Thus, evidence on the role of pension funds for the development of private equity industries and for explaining cross-country variations in private equity investments is mixed.

The ratio of bank assets to firms listed on stock markets does not affect any of the measures of venture capital and private equity investments. This is in line with the results presented in Schertler (2004). According to this study, neither banks' profitability calculated as profits over assets nor banks' assets over stock market capitalization help in explaining early-stage investments.

Returns in stock market segments for fast-growing firms affect the annual percentage changes in private equity investments significantly positive. The sizes of the coefficients of stock market returns depend on the measure of private equity investments. The coefficient in the early-stage investment equation is about 60 per cent higher than the coefficients in the other equations. This positive effect of stock market returns has also been documented in Schertler (2005b). Moreover, using US data, Gompers and Lerner (1999b) have found that the previous year's equity market return has a positive effect on the number of investments but not on the volume of investments. Using a panel dataset similar to the one used here, Da Rin *et al.* (2004) have found evidence that the ratio of early-stage investments to total private equity investments depends positively on a dummy variable which is equal to one if a stock market for fast-growing firms is available in a particular country, and zero otherwise.

In addition, the empirical results presented in Table 6.2 show that private equity investments do not only depend on the returns in stock market segments for fast-growing firms but also on the volatility of the returns in stock market segments for fast-growing firms. The volatility of stock market returns has a larger impact on early-stage investments than on early- and expansion-stage investments and private equity investments. Thus, when returns in stock markets for fast-growing firms increase substantially, private equity companies invest more in firms' early stages of development than in later stages.

Regarding European governments, new funds provided by governments have a significantly positive impact on the number of early-stage investments, and, at a lower significance level, on the volume of private equity investments. This is in line with the evidence presented in Leleux and Surlemont (2003). They have analysed the impact of governments' funding on private equity investments. They have studied whether government funds seed the industry or whether they crowd out non-government-related private equity funds. Their results using Granger causality test support neither the seed nor the crowding out hypotheses. Leleux and Surlemont have argued that government funds seem to be the consequence of developments in the private equity industry.

Capital gains tax rates help in explaining cross-country differences in private equity investments. In line with my expectations I find that the higher the capital gains tax rate, the lower the percentage change in the number of early-stage investments. Thus, higher capital gains tax rates lower incentives to provide capital to firms at their early stage of development. However, it is puzzling that the capital gains tax rate has a positive, albeit insignificant, impact on the volume and number of early- and expansion-stage investments and on private equity investments.

The legal environment also helps in explaining cross-country variations in private equity investments. The countries' legal tradition has a negative impact on all the measures of private equity investments, albeit it is only significant for the percentage change in private equity investments. In unreported regressions, I tested two additional legal environment indicators. According to these regressions, anti-director rights have a significantly positive impact on the percentage change in the number of early-stage investments. Moreover, accounting standards have a significantly positive effect on the percentage change in the volume of early-stage investments. By contrast, Jeng and Wells (2000) have found a negative and significant impact of accounting standards on early- and expansion-stage investments. In their study, they have argued that an insignificant coefficient could be explained by the fact that empirical proxies used for accounting standards are those of publicly listed firms and not of privately held firms. However, they have not offered any explanation for the significantly negative coefficient in their study.

Regarding measures of entrepreneurial environment, the human capital endowment of the countries plays an important role for early-stage investments. Specifically, the growth rate in patent applications to the European patent office has a significantly positive impact on the volume and number of early-stage investments. This is in line with the evidence presented in Schertler (2005b) and Romain and van Pottelsberghe (2004). Schertler (2005b) has shown that the number of patent applications to the US patent office, the number of R&D researchers, and the gross expenditures on R&D help in explaining early-stage investments, and to a lesser extent early- and expansion-stage investments. Romain and van Pottelsberghe (2004) have shown positive effects of business R&D expenditures on early-stage investments.

Employment protection neither affects the early-stage investments, nor early- and expansion-stage investments nor private equity investments significantly. The empirical impact of labour market regulation on venture capital investments has also been analysed by Jeng and Wells (2000), who have found evidence that labour market rigidities have a significantly negative impact on early-stage investments, but not on early- and expansion-stage investments. This difference in their results can be driven by several factors. First, Jeng and Wells used a measure of labour market rigidity that differs from the one I used here. Second, the study by Jeng and Wells is based on a different country sample and a different time period. Third, Jeng and Wells ignored several variables I used here, such as measures of the countries' human capital endowments, and, in addition, I did not use several variables that Jeng and Wells included in their study, such as the amount of initial public offerings.

In unreported regressions, I tested whether my other measures of entrepreneurship, the firm creation index, and the entrepreneurship index, help in explaining early-stage investments, early- and expansion-stage investments and private equity investments. However, estimations give no significant results. Most importantly, however, the inclusion of these variables does not change the coefficients and significance levels of the other variables in a substantial way.

Macroeconomic conditions, captured by the short-term interest rate, do not help in explaining the percentage change in either early-stage investments, or early- and expansion-stage investments or private equity investments. The growth rate of GDP has only a significantly positive effect on the number of private equity investments, but not on venture capital investments. In contrast to my estimation results, Gompers and Lerner (1999b), Schertler (2005b) and Romain and van

Pottelsberghe (2004) have found a pro-cyclical behaviour of venture capital investments. Gompers and Lerner (1999b) have found that the growth of gross state products leads to an increase in the state volume of venture capital investments. Using a sample similar to the one used here, Schertler (2005b) has found a significantly positive impact only in some specifications, while Romain and van Pottelsberghe (2004) have found a significantly positive coefficient of the growth rate in GDP in all their model specifications. These different results regarding macroeconomic conditions may be the result of different constructions of the endogenous variables. More specifically, Schertler (2005b) has used first differences of investments relative to GDP, while Romain and van Pottelsberghe (2004) have used investments relative to GDP.

Robustness check

The above discussion has shown that evidence on potential determinants of cross-country variations of private equity investments varies slightly from study to study. These differences can stem from at least four sources. First, the construction of the endogenous variables differs fundamentally among the studies mentioned, that is, depending whether the studies used investment levels relative to GDP, first-differences of investment levels relative to GDP, shares of early-stage investments relative to private equity investments or annual growth rates of private equity investments. Second, the number and type of exogenous variables included in the regression equations differ substantially. Third, the time frame under consideration differs. Fourth, the methodologies applied vary from static panel estimations to dynamic panel estimations.

Therefore, I checked the robustness of my estimation results. I did so by excluding the period of time characterized by higher stock prices, that is, the years 1999 to 2001, by excluding the United Kingdom from the sample, and by employing a static fixed effects estimator. My robustness checks are limited in scope because of the few number of countries and time periods included in the panel dataset.[22] Table 6.3 gives the estimation results of my various robustness checks.

I started by estimating my regression equation for percentage changes in early-stage investments for a sample excluding the years 1999 to 2001. As the regression results presented in columns (1) and (2) indicate, some changes take place. The t-values are lower in this sample than in the full sample excepting the t-values of the short-term interest rate. Regarding variables related to financial intermediation and financial markets, I find

Table 6.3 Robustness of determinants of venture capital investments
This table reports robustness checks of determinants of venture capital investments. Estimation results in columns (1) and (2) are based on a sample excluding the years 1999 to 2001. Estimation results in columns (3) and (4) are based on a sample excluding the United Kingdom. GMM estimations with absolute Windmeijer's (2005) corrected t-statistics are shown in columns (1) to (4). Fixed effects estimations are given in columns (5) and (6). *** (**, *) denotes significance at 1 (5, 10) per cent levels.

	(1) SVC	(2) SVCN	(3) SVC	(4) SVCN	(5) SVC	(6) SVCN
Endogenous variable (1)	–0.351*** (3.58)	–0.286*** (3.44)	–0.216** (2.65)	–0.158* (1.82)	–0.432*** (5.26)	–0.275*** (3.27)
Growh rate of new funds (1)	0.048 (0.51)	0.095 (1.47)	–0.055 (0.62)	–0.032 (0.41)	0.096 (1.18)	0.067 (1.13)
New funds by pension funds (1)	0.159 (0.22)	0.809 (1.48)	0.568 (0.83)	0.678 (1.24)	0.03 (0.04)	0.431 (0.71)
Bank assets to listed firms	0 (0.25)	0 (0.61)	0 (0.13)	0 (0.54)	0 (0.72)	0 (0.1)
Stock market returns	–0.671 (0.51)	–0.253 (0.25)	1.365*** (4.06)	1.177*** (4.42)	1.399*** (3.56)	1.149*** (4.02)
Stock market return volatility	0.434** (2.77)	0.276** (2.26)	0.276*** (3.93)	0.184*** (3.43)	0.208** (2.31)	0.144** (2.19)
New funds by governments	0.006 (0.92)	0.009 (1.6)	0.007 (1.06)	0.012 (1.73)	0 (0.02)	0.007 (1.43)
Capital gains tax rate	–0.01 (1.08)	–0.011 (1.29)	–0.011* (1.77)	–0.013** (2.16)	–0.017 (0.7)	–0.019 (1.04)
Law tradition	–0.182 (0.43)	–0.211 (0.86)				
Growth rate of patents (1)	0.888* (1.98)	0.955*** (3.84)	1.657*** (3.27)	1.105*** (4.47)	1.208 (1.61)	0.943* (1.73)
Labour index	–0.046 (0.22)	0.014 (0.12)	0.079 (0.5)	0.078 (0.69)	–0.19 (0.49)	0.12 (0.42)
Short-term interest rate	–0.044 (1.29)	–0.047 (1.72)	–0.043 (0.86)	–0.044 (1.65)	–0.059 (1.35)	–0.049 (1.54)
Growth rate of GDP	1.422 (0.97)	2.238 (1.07)	1.245 (0.92)	1.982 (1.71)	1.994 (0.92)	2.231 (1.41)
Number of observations	99	99	137	137	147	147
Number of countries	16	16	15	15	16	16
F-test	10.2***	43.8***	15.5***	100.4***	4.9***	4.8***
Hansen test (p-value)	0.286	0.401	0.181	0.508		
AR1 (p-value)	0.041	0.006	0.019	0.005		
AR2 (p-value)	0.706	0.864	0.705	0.823		
R^2 (within)	0.33	0.33				

Source: see Table A3.

that stock market returns no longer help in explaining the growth in early-stage investments, while the volatility of stock market returns has a positive and significant effect on the growth rate of early-stage investments. The coefficient of the capital gains tax rate keeps its magnitude but loses significance. As in the full sample, the growth rate in patents has a positive and significant impact on the percentage change in early-stage investments. The coefficients of the short-term interest rate keep their signs and have higher t-values.

Moreover, I estimated my model for a sample excluding the United Kingdom, because the British economy is more market-based than the other European countries considered here (Beck and Levine 2002). Results are reported in columns (3) and (4) of Table 6.3. Excluding the United Kingdom from the sample does not change the results with respect to the variables capturing financial intermediations and financial markets. The coefficients of stock market returns and stock market return volatility change neither size nor the t-values substantially. The capital gains tax rate again has a negative and significant effect on the percentage change in early-stage investments. The percentage change in patents again has a positive and significant effect on the percentage change in early-stage investments. Thus, excluding the United Kingdom from the panel dataset does not offer any new insights. All the coefficients considered in the analysis keep their signs and significance levels.

In another robustness check, I employed a static fixed effect panel estimator. Because of the endogenous lagged variable included in the regression, results based on the fixed effects model are biased (Nickell 1981, Kiviet 1995). Results are reported in columns (5) and (6) of Table 6.3. The static panel estimator yields similar qualitative results. Stock market returns, the volatility of stock market returns and increases in the number of patents have a significantly positive impact on the percentage change in early-stage investments. The capital gains tax rate keeps its sign but loses significance.

The robustness checks reveal that neither excluding the years 1999 to 2001 nor excluding the United Kingdom from the sample, nor using a static panel estimator, changes my estimation results for determinants explaining cross-country variations in early-stage investments substantially. Specifically, stock market developments, captured by the stock market returns for fast-growing firms and the volatility of these stock market returns, and the countries' human capital endowments, captured by the growth in patents, help in explaining the percentage changes in early-stage investments.

Summary

The analysis presented in this chapter has partly confirmed previous studies on the determinants of cross-country variations in venture capital and private equity investments. In addition, the empirical analysis has offered new insights on the determinants of cross-country variations. Regarding confirming earlier estimation results, the analysis has shown that new funds provided by pension funds and governments, capital gains taxes, the countries' legal environment and the countries' human capital endowments play a role for the developments in private equity industries. Regarding identifying new determinants, the analysis has shown that not only returns in stock markets for fast-growing firms help in explaining venture capital investments, but that the volatility of these stock market returns is a significant factor for venture capital investments.

7
Industry Specialization

This chapter deals with comparative advantages in the production of goods and services and whether these comparative advantages are related to private equity investments available in a country. Thus, this chapter deepens the discussion of the industry features of private equity industries and the industry structure of private equity investments introduced in Chapter 4.

The first part of this chapter describes comparative advantages of European countries in selected industries. The second part discusses why there might be a link between private equity investments available in a country, and comparative advantages, and uses a country panel dataset to shed some light on the link between private equity investments and comparative advantages in these industries.

Comparative advantages in selected industries

Since I have already described the industry structure of private equity investments in Chapter 4, I start here by discussing the comparative advantages of European countries in those industries preferred by private equity companies. A measure of industry specialization in the production of goods is the following ratio proposed by Balassa (1986):

$$b_{ijt} = \frac{X_{ijt} - M_{ijt}}{X_{ijt} + M_{ijt}} \tag{7.1}$$

where M_{ijt} denotes imports of goods produced in industry j of country i at time t, and X_{ijt} denotes exports of industry j and country i at time t. Country i is specialized in the production of goods produced in industry j if b_{ijt} is positive.

Panel (a) of Table 7.1 offers information on b_{ijt} for European countries in those industries in which private equity companies prefer to invest, averaged over the years 1991 to 2002. As in Chapter 4, I distinguish seven industries: information and communications (IT), biotechnology and medicine (BIO), energy (ENERGY), agriculture and consumer-related products (AGRICULTURE), transportation and industrial products (TRANSPORTATION), chemicals and materials (CHEMICAL), and industrial automation (IA). Table A4 gives information on sources and aggregation details for exports, imports and production in these industries.

Overall, European countries were not often specialized in the industries in which private equity companies mainly invest. Regarding the IT industry, only two countries, Finland and Sweden, had a comparative advantage in this industry during the observation period. Finland's comparative advantage in the IT industry might be the result of NOKIA's investment activities in this industry. NOKIA has also provided substantial amounts of capital for private equity investments. Sweden's comparative advantage is with 0.024 very low.

Six countries, Belgium, Denmark, France, Germany, Sweden and the United Kingdom had a comparative advantage in the BIO industry. To some extent, these comparative advantages were driven by government interventions. For example, the German government launched the BioRegio contest, which aimed at strengthening research focusing on biotechnology (Engel 2002). Its objective was to develop regional concepts on the potential of commercializing the biotechnology industry in the German regions.

Regarding the ENERGY industry, which is a relatively old industry compared to the IT and BIO industry, Norway and the United Kingdom were the only countries with a comparative advantage in this industry. Note, that Norway's comparative advantage in the ENERGY industry was several times larger than the United Kingdom's comparative advantage, which is likely to be a result of the significant availability of natural energy resources in Norway.

In the AGRICULTURE industry, Denmark and, to a lesser extent, the Netherlands had a comparative advantage, while many other countries, such as Italy, Portugal and the United Kingdom had a substantial comparative disadvantage. In the Netherlands the comparative advantage in this industry varied only slightly over time, while in Denmark the comparative advantage declined from 0.36 in 1991 to less than 0.27 in 2002.

In the TRANSPORTATION industry, Italy and Germany had substantial comparative advantages, while Greece, Portugal and Norway had substantial comparative disadvantages. Italy's comparative advantage in this industry steadily increased in the beginning of the 1990s up to 0.33 in 1996. Thereafter, it steadily declined to a value of 0.17 in 2002. By contrast, Germany's comparative advantage in this industry increased from 0.25 in 1991 to about 0.37 in 2002. Greece's comparative disadvantage varied a little over time and Portugal's comparative disadvantage was reduced substantially from –0.57 in 1991 to –0.19 in 2002, while Norway's comparative disadvantage reached, with a value of –0.46, a peak in 1998.

In the CHEMICAL industry, only Germany had a comparative advantage, while Greece and Portugal had a comparative disadvantage. Germany's comparative advantage varied slightly over time, while Greece's and Portugal's comparative disadvantage declined over time. In Greece, b_{ijt} changed from –0.71 in 1991 to –0.59 in 2002. In Portugal, b_{ijt} changed from –0.50 in 1991 to –0.42 in 2002.

In the IA industry, Germany and Denmark had a comparative advantage, while Greece and Portugal had a comparative disadvantage. Germany's comparative advantage increased from 0.17 in 1991 to more than 0.25 in 2002, while Denmark's comparative advantage in this industry varied only slightly over time. Greece's comparative disadvantage was reduced over time from –0.91 in 1991 to –0.79 in 2002, while Portugal's comparative disadvantage varied in both directions over time.

An alternative indicator for industrial specialization is the ratio between production and consumption proposed by Gustavson *et al.* (1999):

$$r_{ijt} = \frac{Q_{ijt}}{C_{ijt}} = \frac{Q_{ijt}}{Q_{ijt} - X_{ijt} + M_{ijt}} \tag{7.2}$$

where Q_{ijt} denotes production in industry j of country i at time t and C_{ijt} denotes consumption. Country i is a net importer (exporter) of goods produced in industry j if r_{ijt} is smaller (larger) than one. Panel (b) of Table 7.1 reports comparative advantages for the various industries and European countries based on r_{ijt}. Overall, the comparative advantages on r_{ijt} are in line with the comparative advantages based on b_{ijt}.

The above discussion of comparative advantages has shown that some countries strengthened their comparative advantages over time, while others lost their comparative advantages in the industries under consideration. In order to test whether there is a joint time trend in the development of comparative advantages and disadvantages of

Table 7.1 Comparative advantages in Europe

This panel reports $b_{ijt} = (X_{ijt} - M_{ijt})/(X_{ijt} + M_{ijt})$, averaged over the years 1991 to 2002. Time trend is the coefficient of a time trend in a fixed effects model including year dummies, where b_{ijt} is the endogenous variable. *** (**) denotes significance at the 1 (5) per cent level.

Panel (a)

	IT	BIO	ENERGY	AGRICULTURE	TRANSPORTATION	CHEMICAL	IA
Austria	–0.070	–0.125	–0.778	–0.057	–0.027	–0.125	–0.188
Belgium	–0.058	0.076	–0.320	0.026	0.031	0.077	–0.189
Denmark	–0.149	0.417	–0.062	0.314	–0.018	–0.139	0.243
Finland	0.124	–0.416	–0.503	0.146	0.049	–0.137	0.037
France	–0.030	0.115	–0.648	0.124	0.111	0.070	–0.063
Germany	–0.036	0.204	–0.691	–0.251	0.326	0.200	0.207
Greece	–0.704	–0.753	–0.476	–0.136	–0.847	–0.640	–0.840
Italy	–0.130	–0.063	–0.651	–0.276	0.229	–0.136	–0.141
Netherlands	–0.033	0.003	–0.015	0.245	–0.106	0.147	0.075
Norway	–0.460	–0.209	0.924	0.137	–0.364	–0.007	–0.328
Portugal	–0.196	–0.627	na	–0.318	–0.383	–0.471	–0.573
Spain	–0.300	–0.297	–0.669	–0.040	–0.017	–0.210	–0.535
Sweden	0.024	0.414	–0.427	–0.068	na	–0.170	0.040
United Kingdom	–0.063	0.185	0.170	–0.317	–0.034	0.025	0.012
Time Trend	0.010***	0.004**	0.006**	0.002	0.007***	0.007***	0.011***

Table 7.1 Comparative advantages in Europe – *continued*

This panel reports $r_{ijt} = Q_{ijt} \;/\; (Q_{ijt} - X_{ijt} + M_{ijt})$, averaged over the years 1991 to 2002. Time trend is the coefficient of a time trend in a fixed effects model including year dummies, where r_{ijt} is the endogenous variable. *** denotes significance at the 1 per cent level.

Panel (b)

	IT	BIO	ENERGY	AGRICULTURE	TRANSPORTATION	CHEMICAL	IA
Austria	0.905	0.815	0.566	0.979	0.966	0.841	0.714
Belgium	0.869	1.213	0.667	1.032	1.102	1.172	0.554
Denmark	0.750	2.080	0.952	1.267	0.975	0.830	1.625
Finland	1.172	0.602	0.621	1.041	1.054	0.888	1.040
France	0.970	1.070	na	1.044	1.101	1.065	0.955
Germany	0.965	1.289	0.627	0.917	1.340	1.169	1.248
Greece	0.377	0.394	0.713	0.957	0.264	0.544	0.176
Italy	0.908	0.974	0.679	0.927	1.248	0.919	0.878
Netherlands	0.890	1.004	0.989	1.247	0.844	1.273	1.599
Norway	0.515	0.770	na	1.046	0.677	na	0.667
Portugal	0.755	0.656	na	0.905	0.570	0.675	0.368
Spain	0.747	0.851	0.642	0.995	0.986	0.872	0.552
Sweden	1.054	1.681	0.598	0.979	na	0.822	1.042
United Kingdom	0.910	1.207	1.087	0.902	0.971	1.020	1.017
Time Trend	0.140***	0.062***	0.002	0.000	0.009***	0.009***	0.0137

Source: see Table A4.

European countries in the selected industries, I used fixed-effects regressions of b_{ijt} and r_{ijt} and I included a time trend. According to the coefficients of the time trend, which are reported in Panel (a) and Panel (b) of Table 7.1, there is a significantly positive time trend in several industries. When I used b_{ijt}, I found a significantly positive time trend in comparative advantages for the IT industry, the BIO industry, the ENERGY industry, the TRANSPORTATION industry, the CHEMICAL industry and the IA industry. When I used r_{ijt}, I found a significantly positive time trend in comparative advantages for the IT industry, the BIO industry, the TRANSPORTATION industry, and the CHEMICAL industry but not for the ENERGY industry and the IA industry. Thus, the two indicators for comparative advantages, b_{ijt} and r_{ijt}, show different developments for some industries over time. However, for the IT, the BIO, the TRANSPORTATION and the CHEMICAL industries both indicators give evidence for a positive time trend for European countries. This means that European countries have, on average, improved their comparative position *vis-à-vis* other countries during the observation period. This development in comparative advantages over time might be related to the development in private equity investments, which increased substantially over time. To this issue I turn next.

Private equity finance as a source of comparative advantages

According to traditional trade theory, a country well endowed with a specific production factor specializes in producing goods that use this production factor intensively. A production factor can, however, only give rise to comparative advantages if it is internationally immobile. In the case of financial markets, in general, credit contract enforcement by domestic institutions may give rise to comparative advantages in those industries that rely heavily on such financing (Kletzer and Bardhan 1987). Comparative advantages based on financial markets may also be due to the risk diversification function of financial markets (Baldwin 1989).

In the case of private equity industries in particular, the control mechanisms used by private equity companies to mitigate adverse selection and moral hazard problems may give rise to comparative advantages in particular industries. Although private equity finance has been globalized in recent years (see the discussion in the next chapter), it is to some extent immobile because of the active involvement of the private equity companies in the form of management support and monitoring services. Recent empirical studies have discussed the role of distance in private equity industries. They have documented that the monitoring and management support of private equity companies decreases with the distance between the private equity company and portfolio firms. Thus, while one part of private equity finance, the capital, is likely to be internationally mobile, the more important part of private equity and especially venture capital finance, the monitoring and management support services provided to portfolio firms by experienced venture capital companies specialized in selected industries and development stages, is not.

Recent literature has analysed whether financial sector development helps in explaining industry specialization patterns in the production of goods. Rajan and Zingales (1998) and Demigüc-Kunt and Maksimovic (1998) have found that those industries using more external funding for their investments grow faster in those countries in which capital markets are highly developed. Using an OECD dataset, Svaleryd and Vlachos (2005) have found evidence that the financial sector has more power in explaining specialization in industries among OECD countries than differences in human or physical capital. In their analysis, they have used a cross-country dataset without a time dimension, and have estimated the impact of human capital endowment, physical capital endowment and financial sector development indicators on r_{ij} under the assumption that the resource needs in the industries are identical for all countries under consideration.

In the following, I discuss whether private equity investments as an endowment factor of European countries help in explaining comparative advantages in selected industries in Europe. In order to shed light on the link between comparative advantages and private equity investments, I used the data from the EVCA statistics. I had data on 14 countries for 11 years. The number of observations in the empirical analysis, however, varies over industries because of data availability for exports, imports, and productions. My empirical model, which I based on the indicator proposed by Gustavson *et al.* (1999), has the following form:

$$\Delta r_{ijt} = \beta_{1j} + \beta_{2j}\Delta PE_{it} + \beta_{3j}\Delta SMC_{it} + \beta_{4j}\Delta BC_{it} + \beta_{5j}\Delta HC_{it} + C_{ij} + \varepsilon_{ijt} \quad (7.3)$$
$$\textit{for each } j$$

where Δ denotes percentage changes, PE_{it} denotes private equity investments in country i at time t, SMC_{it} denotes stock market capitalization, BC_{it} denotes asset holdings of banks, and HC_{it} denotes the human capital endowment approximated by the number of research and development employees in the business and government sector, C_{ij} denotes country-specific effects for industry j, and e_{ijt} is the error term. Table A4 provides details on the variables used. I used percentage changes of the variables because most of the variables under consideration are non-stationary. I estimated (7.3) separately for each industry under consideration.

Thus, my estimation strategy differs from the one used in recent literature (see, for example, Svaleryd and Vlachos 2005). More specifically, I did not use cross-country regressions but rather a panel approach to analyse the role of private equity investments for comparative advantages in selected industries. Moreover, I did not use input requirements of the industries. In cross-country regressions, the information on input requirements of the industries is necessary to account for differences across industries with respect to their dependence on endowment, which is necessary to take into account that an increase in the country's human capital endowment has a larger impact on, for example, the biotechnology industry than on the agriculture industry. In cross-country regressions, the information on input requirements of the industries comes from other sources (usually this information is based on a single country and then applied to all other countries in the sample). Therefore, the coefficients I estimated do capture not only the response of the industry to changes in factor endowments but also the input requirements of the industry.

Table 7.2 presents estimation results for equation 7.3 for each industry. The overall R^2 indicates that the specifications have little explanatory power although I included year dummies in each specification. The comparative advantage or disadvantage in the ENERGY, AGRICULTURE, TRANSPORTATION and IA industry is not affected by the countries' private equity investments. However, the comparative advantage in two industries under consideration depends significantly positive on private equity investments. More specifically, private equity investments have a significantly positive effect on the comparative advantage in the BIO and the CHEMICAL industries. Thus, private equity investments increase the output in the BIO industry and in the CHEMICAL industries. Only a part of this output increase is consumed at home, the rest is consumed abroad. For the IT industry, a similar effect holds, only at a lower significance level.

The other variables included in the regressions do not help in explaining Europe's comparative advantages. Percentage changes in asset holdings of banks affect the comparative advantages in the IT industry positively at a significance level of 11 per cent. This is

Table 7.2 Explaining comparative advantages for selected industries

This table reports estimation results using a fixed effects regression models allowing for a AR(1) structure in error terms. Endogenous variables are percentage changes of $r_{ijt} = Q_{ijt}/(Q_{ijt} - X_{ijt} + M_{ijt})$. All variables are in percentage changes. Year dummies are included in each regression. Absolute AR(1) and heteroscedastic-consistent t-statistics are given below the coefficients. *** (**, *) denotes significance at the 1 (5, 10) per cent level.

	(1) IT	(2) BIO	(3) ENERGY	(4) AGRICULTURE	(5) TRANSPORTATION	(6) CHEMICAL	(7) IA
PE investments	0.019	0.037*	–0.014	–0.002	–0.017	0.018*	–0.032
	(1.4)	(1.95)	(0.64)	(0.72)	(0.82)	(1.74)	(0.74)
Bank assets	0.128	0.121	–0.201	–0.008	0.099	0	0.275
	(1.62)	(1.01)	(1.23)	(0.49)	(1.02)	(0)	(1.15)
Stock market	0.070**	–0.111**	–0.002	0.008	–0.013	–0.055**	0.087
capitalization	(2.15)	(2.33)	(0.03)	(1.27)	(0.34)	(2.08)	(0.84)
Research employees	–0.053	0.081	–0.153	–0.015	–0.237*	0.054	–0.082
	(0.47)	(0.49)	(0.64)	(0.58)	(1.75)	(0.66)	(0.23)
Constant	–0.051***	–0.005	–0.008	0.003	–0.002	–0.004	–0.012
	(2.81)	(0.21)	(0.27)	(0.71)	(0.07)	(0.28)	(0.19)
Number of observations	105	109	72	99	97	100	105
Number of countries	14	14	10	13	13	13	14
F-test	2.184	1.065	0.767	2.386	2.077	1.622	1.002
Overall R^2	0.153	0.142	0.101	0.242	0.269	0.175	0.106

Source: see Table A4.

astonishing, since firms in this industry are believed to have limited access to bank credits. Thus, an increase in the endowment of this factor should not foster comparative advantages in this industry. Percentage changes in stock market capitalization have a positive and significant impact on comparative advantages in the IT industry. Moreover, percentage changes in stock market capitalization significantly decrease the percentage changes in comparative advantages in the BIO industry and the CHEMICAL industry. Percentage changes in research and development employees used as a measure of the countries' human capital endowment have a negative and significant impact on the percentage changes in the comparative advantage of the CHEMICAL industry.

These results give only an indication of the link between comparative advantages in the industries of European countries and private equity investments for several reasons. First, I built my estimations on each industry separately instead of using the full industry spectrum of European countries or even OECD countries. Thus, I have not used all information available. Second, while bank assets and stock market capitalization are stock variables, I captured the countries' private equity endowments by using a flow variable. From a theoretical point of view, such a measure is inadequate. From an empirical point of view, however, data on private equity flows are the only measure available. Third, there might be a severe endogeneity problem involved in the estimation: Incentives for individuals and capital providers to start specialized private equity companies might be stronger in those countries that have a comparative advantage in those industries in which firms are very likely to demand private equity or venture capital finance for their start-ups. Thus, private equity investments may be the result of the countries' comparative advantages in particular industries, and not the source of the countries' comparative advantages.

Generally, the role of private equity companies in the creation of new industries, in their dependence on these industries and their role in changing the face of existing industries has received little attention in the academic arena. While the literature has analysed criteria used by private equity companies in the selection of portfolio firms, it has largely ignored the intertemporal interdependencies that might exist in the selection process. The selection process might be either supply-side or demand-side driven. Regarding the supply-side, one might argue that the help of private equity companies in commercializing products may create a technology push in the economy. Then, recent developments in the IT industry might be, to some extent, the result of private equity companies having created promising investment opportunities for their capital providers. Regarding the demand-side, one might argue that the help of private equity companies in commercializing products might be the result of changes in consumer preferences that are identified earlier, or perhaps only expected, by venture capital and private equity companies. These issues have, however, not been addressed by the recent literature. They might be at the focus of research within the next decades.

Summary

The empirical analysis presented in this chapter has offered first insights into the link between countries' comparative advantages and the availability of private equity investments. It has found a significant link between comparative advantages in the BIO and CHEMICAL industries and the countries' private equity investments. However, for other industries, such as the TRANSPORTATION industry, the analysis has not found a significant link. This chapter has shown a significant need for future research with respect to the role that private equity companies take on in creating new industries, and changing the face of old industries.

8 Internationalization

This chapter deals with internationalization strategies in Europe's private equity industries. In the boom at the end of the 1990s, substantial amounts of private equity flowed across countries. Thus, like other financial segments, such as the banking industry, private equity industries have become more internationalized. This chapter focuses on the microeconomics of venture capital finance when analysing internationalization strategies of private equity companies, and it focuses on the industry features of the private equity industries when identifying countries that are net exporters or importers of private equity.

The first part of this chapter describes empirically international private equity flows in Europe. The second part discusses reasons why private equity activity has become more internationalized. The third part uses qualitative micro-data and quantitative macro-data in order to shed light on some of the reasons why private equity industries have internationalized.

Private equity flows

Since the international activities of private equity companies have not been at the focus of the Chapters 3 to 5, I provide an empirical description of the internationalization trends in private equity industries by using the various micro-datasets at hand and the EVCA statistics. Internationalization in private equity industries can take several forms. Generally, four different types of private equity flows can be distinguished. First, domestic private equity companies invest in foreign high-technology firms without the involvement of foreign private equity companies. Second, both foreign and domestic private equity companies invest in domestic high-technology firms. In this case private equity companies syndicate their investments internationally (internationally syndicated investments have been described in Table 4.4). Third, domestic private equity companies invest in foreign private equity funds. In this case private equity companies raise new funds for their investments internationally. Fourth, domestic private equity companies set up foreign private equity companies either by founding their own subsidiaries (Greenfield investment) or by investing in already established companies (merger and acquisition).

Micro-data

A look at the micro-datasets of German and French VC companies indicates that both German and French private equity companies have a propensity to invest abroad. The datasets inform on whether private equity companies are willing to invest abroad, or whether they invest only in domestic firms. Out of 143 German private equity companies, about 34 per cent indicate they would invest abroad. When excluding the 16 government-based private equity companies, which invest only in German firms, about 39 per cent of the German private equity companies indicate they would invest abroad. Of 96 French private equity companies, excluding government-based private equity companies, about 50 per cent indicate they would invest abroad. Thus, the propensity to invest in a foreign firm is somewhat higher for the French than for the German private equity companies.

The VCPro dataset also informs on the private equity companies' propensity to invest abroad. Additionally, it informs on the countries in which private equity companies are willing to invest. From this information, I constructed two variables. The first variable is a dummy variable that equals one if the private equity company indicates it would invest abroad, and zero otherwise. The second variable measures the number of countries in which a private equity company would invest. This number is equal to one if the private equity company would invest only in one country, while it is equal to 18 if the private equity company has no geographical preference at all.

Table 8.1 offers information on these two variables for the European countries under consideration. About 63 per cent of the European private equity companies have a propensity to invest in foreign firms. This propensity varies across countries. In Ireland and Portugal only 22 per cent of the private equity companies indicate that they would invest in foreign firms. By contrast, in Switzerland and Norway, more than 80 per cent of the private equity companies indicate that they would invest in foreign firms.

Table 8.1 Propensity of private equity companies to invest abroad
This table reports the propensity of European private equity companies to invest abroad. The percentage of private equity companies denotes the percentage of private equity companies that indicated they would invest abroad. The number of countries denotes the number of countries in which the private equity company would invest in. The maximum number of countries is 18. Mean test reports the t-statistic of a mean test on equality of the number of countries compared to the number of countries in which British private equity companies indicated they would invest. *** (**, *) denotes significance at the 1 (5, 10) per cent level.

	Percentage of private equity companies	Mean number of countries	Mean test
Austria	56.00	7.16	1.43
Belgium	79.41	10.44	–0.72
Denmark	69.23	7.58	1.25
Finland	61.76	8.62	0.59
France	75.00	11.61	–2.00**
Germany	63.87	9.00	0.52
Greece	72.73	10.09	–0.25
Ireland	22.22	2.06	7.11***
Italy	50.00	8.36	0.61
Netherlands	75.76	10.00	–0.38
Norway	84.21	6.63	1.98*
Portugal	22.22	2.78	3.58***
Spain	33.33	4.00	4.07***
Sweden	44.05	4.36	6.18***
Switzerland	93.18	14.05	–4.37***
United Kingdom	62.38	9.47	–
Total	62.76	8.65	

Source: VCPro dataset, own calculations.

According to Table 8.1, the average number of countries in which private equity companies would invest is nine. Again, there are substantial variations across countries. In order to test whether these variations are statistically significant, I used an unpaired mean test of equality of the mean number of countries in which British private equity companies indicated they would invest as compared to the number in which private equity companies in other countries indicated they would invest. The test results indicate that the mean number of countries in which portfolio firms can be located is significantly higher for private equity companies located in France and Switzerland than in the United Kingdom. In addition, the mean number of countries in which portfolio firms can be located is significantly lower for private equity companies located in Ireland, Norway, Portugal, Spain and Sweden than for private equity companies located in the United Kingdom.

The largest international European player is *3i*, which is headquartered in the United Kingdom and has offices in Austria, Denmark, Finland, France and in many other European countries. The largest international buy-out and development capital company is *Schröder Ventures*, which is also headquartered in the United Kingdom. In the mid-1990s, 80 investment professionals in ten countries advised 23 funds (Bingham *et al.* 1998). One out of 23 funds was an international fund, while 22 funds were focused on one country only. The interaction between the advisers of the various country-focused funds was low (Bingham *et al.* 1998).

US venture capital companies, such as *Advent*, *General Atlantic* and *Benchmark*, entered European private equity markets systematically in the boom phase at the end of the 1990s (Hardymon *et al.* 2003). They entered European markets for several reasons: to diversify (although the return correlation between Europe and the United States is high), to avoid competition, which had become stronger in the United States, and to find promising early-stage deals (Hardymon *et al.* 2003). Most US venture capital companies entered Europe through the United Kingdom, because it is also an English-speaking country with a market-based financial system. However, business models differed between US venture capital companies and European (British) private equity companies. While European companies focused mainly on financial statements, US companies focused on the potential of technological ideas and the team of the portfolio firm involved (Hardymon *et al.* 2003). The entrance of US venture capital companies may have engendered a change in the business model used by European companies towards an increasing focus on technological ideas in addition to financial statements.

Aggregated data

While the micro-datasets inform only on the propensity of private equity companies to invest abroad, the EVCA statistics provide information on the amounts of funds raised and invested abroad. Based on the EVCA statistics, Table 8.2 informs on the internationally raised funds as a percentage of total new funds raised, on the volumes of international investments as a percentage of the total volume of investments, and on the number of international investments as a percentage of the total number of investments.[23] Data presented are averages over the years 1991 to 2003.

Table 8.2 Private equity flows
This table reports internationally raised private equity funds and international investments, averaged over the years 1991 to 2003. Internationally raised funds are a percentage of new funds raised. International investment volumes are a percentage of total investment volumes. International investment numbers are a percentage of total investment numbers. Average investment volumes are in 1,000 of euros. Time trend is the coefficient of a time trend in a fixed effects model including year dummies, where private equity flows is the endogenous variable. *** denotes significance at the 1 per cent level.

					Average investment volume	
	Raised funds	Investment volume	Investment number	Rank	at home	abroad
Austria	34.5	18.7	20.9	3	411.6	614.7
Belgium	12.0	22.5	30.5	2	1148.7	853.4
Denmark	12.9	10.9	9.0	9	673.7	843.6
Finland	6.7	13.6	6.4	11	405.0	1029.5
France	20.4	11.9	9.2	8	816.9	1145.0
Germany	30.4	9.6	6.3	12	1071.2	1766.0
Ireland	15.9	9.3	6.2	13	585.5	971.2
Italy	29.2	10.6	6.7	10	2561.5	4416.7
Netherlands	10.0	22.1	15.7	4	1241.0	2186.3
Norway	3.2	13.6	15.2	5	757.0	975.5
Portugal	3.4	3.9	2.9	15	648.3	1255.8
Spain	47.4	3.0	4.7	14	1240.5	1171.9
Sweden	35.5	23.7	11.4	7	1656.4	5388.7
Switzerland	16.2	58.2	54.3	1	1586.8	1915.9
United Kingdom	40.8	19.6	15.0	6	2282.3	3621.6
Time trend	3.96***	1.26***	0.38			

Source: EVCA (various issues), own calculations.

Internationally raised new funds accounted for 21 per cent of total new funds, on average. Countries that raised substantial amounts of new funds abroad were Spain, the United Kingdom and Sweden. In Spain, for example, more than 47 per cent of all new funds came from abroad. By contrast, in Finland, Portugal and Norway, internationally raised new funds accounted for less than 10 per cent. In Norway, for example, little more than 3 per cent of all new funds came from abroad.

International investments accounted for 17 per cent of all investments, on average. In Switzerland, Sweden, and Belgium, the Netherlands and the United Kingdom, private equity companies invested substantially in firms located in foreign countries. In Switzerland, private equity companies invested as much as 58 per cent of the private equity investments abroad. In Sweden Belgium, the Netherlands and the United Kingdom, private equity companies invested approximately 20 per cent of the total investments abroad. Thus, in the United Kingdom and Sweden, private equity companies raised substantial amounts of new funds abroad, and, at the same time, they had substantial investments abroad. In contrast, countries in which private equity companies did not invest substantially in foreign countries were Spain, Germany, Portugal and Ireland. While in Spain private equity companies raised large amounts of new funds internationally, they invested only 3 per cent of the total private equity investments abroad. This might indicate large private equity inflows into Spain. I will come back to this below.

On average, the numbers of international investments, which accounted for 14 per cent of all investments, was lower than the percentage of the volumes of international investments. This indicates that the average volume of investments in foreign firms was larger than the average volume of investments in domestic firms. Overall, differences between volumes and numbers of international investments were small. The exceptions were Finland and Sweden. In the case of Finland and Sweden, volumes of international investments overstated the degree of internationalization in private equity investments. In Sweden, for example, volumes of international investments accounted for 24 per cent of total investments. By contrast, the number of international investments accounted for only 11 per cent of the total number of investments. Thus, a few large deals dominated the international business.

Interestingly, in the case of Norway, Spain and Austria, the percentage of the volumes of international investments was lower than the percentage of the numbers. However, the difference between volumes and numbers was comparatively small. In Austria, for example, the volumes of international investments accounted for about 19 per cent, while the numbers of international investments accounted for 21 per cent.

Combining the information on internationally raised funds and international investments, four different country types can be distinguished. First, those countries in which private equity companies raised some new funds internationally and which made some investments abroad. Finland, Denmark, Ireland and France belong to this group. Second, those countries in which private equity companies raised substantial amounts of new funds abroad but invested only comparatively small amounts of their investments abroad. The United Kingdom, Austria, Italy, Germany and Spain belong to this group. Third, those countries in which private equity companies raised only small amounts of new funds abroad and invested intensively abroad. Belgium, the Netherlands, Switzerland and Norway belong to this group. Fourth, those countries in which private equity companies neither raised substantial new funds abroad nor invested substantial amounts abroad. Portugal belongs to this group of countries.

In order to give an impression of internationalization over time, I ran fixed-effects regressions including a time trend where the endogenous variable is the share of either internationally raised funds, or the number or volume of investments in foreign firms as a percentage of the total investments. The coefficients of the time trend are reported in Table 8.2. In the case of internationally raised funds, as well as in the case of the volume of international investments, the coefficients of the time trend are positive and highly significant, indicating a change in the behaviour of private equity companies from being domestically oriented companies towards being international players.

The EVCA statistics presented so far, do not allow net inflows or outflows to be calculated. However, a recent OECD study has analysed the importance of international private equity flows in 1999 (Baygan and Freudenberg 2000). According to this study, the United Kingdom was the biggest private equity exporter, followed by Belgium and the Netherlands. British private equity companies invested 33 per cent of the British private equity investments in firms in other European and non-European countries. European private equity companies outside of the United Kingdom invested capital, in return, in British firms. This capital inflow accounted for 5 per cent of the British private equity investments. This led to net outflows of 28 per cent of the British investments. The highest net inflows were realized by Ireland and Denmark, whose economies are rather small compared to the British economy. However, larger economies also had net inflows. Germany's firms received more money from abroad than Germany's private equity companies invested in foreign firms. Table 8.3 presents data for 2001. Countries' positions regarding net positions of private equity in- and outflows changed over time. Interestingly, however, the United Kingdom was also the most important private equity exporter in 2001, while Ireland received net inflows of private equity. Moreover, Table 8.3 reveals that Spain realized indeed positive net private equity flows.

Table 8.3 Cross-border private equity investment flows
This table reports cross-border private equity investment flows in 2001 in per cent of domestic investments. Outflows are to other European or non-European countries. Inflows are from other European countries. Total flows are inflows plus outflows. Net flows are inflows minus outflows.

	Outflows	Inflows	Total flows	Net flows
Austria	13	36	49	24
Belgium	91	19	110	–73
Denmark	18	62	80	44
Finland	32	21	53	–12
France	14	10	24	–5
Germany	45	5	50	–40
Ireland	10	16	26	6
Italy	19	2	21	–17
Netherlands	36	8	44	–27
Norway	18	4	22	–14
Spain	3	20	24	17
Sweden	26	10	36	–15
United Kingdom	83	11	94	–71

Source: EVCA (various issues), own calculations.

Reasons for internationalization

The reasons for internationalization in private equity industries are likely, to some extent, to be similar to the reasons of foreign direct investments and portfolio investments in general. Capital flows across borders can have two beneficial effects (Freixas and Rochet 1998). First, consumers can smooth consumption over time and become less dependent on domestic production. Second, firms can borrow from abroad and might thus be able to expand their production. In the case of financial intermediation, diversification gains are a third reason for international capital flows. The determinants of international capital flows in general have been at the center of a host of empirical studies that have focused, for instance, on foreign direct investments of financial intermediaries and on portfolio capital investments.

Regarding foreign direct investments of banks, Focarelli and Pozzolo (1999) have documented that the growth of the host market, the potential for diversification and the degree of openness of the host economy, measured by the volume of bilateral trade, are the most important determinants for foreign direct investments. Apart from these country variables, Focarelli and Pozzolo (1999) have also documented that banking characteristics play an important role. The likelihood of going abroad increases with increases in the efficiency of banks. In a related study, Dahl and Shrieves (1999) have analysed international lending decisions of banks. They have found a complementary relationship between domestic and foreign lending. Barron and Valev (2000) have documented transaction costs, such as information costs, to be significant in international financial flows. They have found evidence that small banks tend to follow large banks. The argument behind this is that smaller banks, being more wealth constrained than larger banks, have fewer incentives to incur the fixed costs of investing in obtaining information on foreign countries in general and foreign firms in particular and thus tend to follow the behaviour of (better informed) larger banks.

Regarding portfolio investments, Portes and Rey (1999) have looked at international equity investments rather than bank lending. Their results about the importance of information costs in a more general sense are informative. Rather than proxy information costs indirectly through a simple distance measure, Portes and Rey have used a number of direct measures such as the volume of telephone calls between two countries or the number of bank branches in the foreign country. Using data on annual equity transaction flows, the authors have found that, after controlling for market size, the information-related variables explain a substantial amount of the cross-sectional variation in equity flows. Return variables are insignificant, thus confirming earlier studies that have rejected the implications of standard portfolio choice models that disregard the impact of information costs or regulations. Finally, Ahearne *et al.* (2004) have shown that variables capturing information costs help in explaining a substantial share of the home bias observed in international investment portfolios.

Apart from these reasons provided by the literature on international capital flows, there are some additional reasons for the internationalization in private equity industries which are specific to these industries. One reason might be that many European countries are too small to generate a sufficient deal flow in a particular high-technology industry. If countries' high-technology industries are too small, private equity companies do not have sufficient investment opportunities to specialize in particular fields of technologies. In this situation they can choose between investing domestically in various industries, implying a lower degree of technological specialization, and investing internationally in a few industries and, thus, being technologically specialized. A second reason might be that more advanced high-technology firms in small European countries demand capital from private equity companies that are internationally active in order to obtain assistance in their efforts to enter foreign product markets and capital markets, for example, *via* an initial public offering on a foreign stock market.

A look at the data

Most of the studies analysing international capital flows make use of bilateral data. Such data are, however, not available for international private equity flows. Therefore, the impact of the growth of the host market, the potential for diversification, and the degree of the openness of the host country on international capital flows cannot be tested for international private equity investments or fundraising with the datasets at hand. However, the datasets at hand allow testing whether the characteristics of private equity companies and the country-specific characteristics are related to international private equity activities.

A few studies have focused on the internationalization in private equity industries. Wright *et al.* (2002) have analysed the risk assessment of domestic and foreign private equity companies in India. Haemmig (2003a, 2003b) has offered a detailed description of private equity flows around the globe. Mäkelä (2004) has investigated cross-border private equity syndicates and the impact of internationalization on portfolio firms. However, to my knowledge, there is no study that analyses the driving forces behind the internationalization strategies of European private equity companies.

Characteristics of private equity companies

A basic characteristic of private equity companies that is likely to matter as regards how internationalized they are is that they specialize in industries and development stages. Industry specialization might increase with internationalization because then diversifying geographically is more relevant to reduce portfolio risks. Reducing portfolio risks by diversifying geographically is more important in the case of industrially specialized than in the case of industrially not specialized private equity companies. Specialization in firms' early stage of development may result in less internationalization because close contacts between venture capital companies and their portfolio firms are necessary to control high risks of early-stage investments.

I measured internationalization using the two variables that I have already described above. My first measure was the number of countries in which private equity companies have a propensity to invest. For this variable, I used the VCPro dataset and employed a NEGBIN model discussed in Chapter 4. My second measure was a dummy variable capturing whether private equity companies are internationally active. For this variable, I used the German and French VC datasets and the VCPro dataset, and employed a LOGIT model. Table A2 provides the definition of the exogenous variables used.

The first two columns of Table 8.4, which are based on the VCPro dataset, present my estimation results. They indicate that the number of countries in which a private equity company has a propensity to invest depends on the volume of funds under management, and on the type of the private equity company. The number of countries increases with the volume of private equity funds under management. Moreover, as the negative and significant coefficients of the dummy variable for specialists indicate, these companies have, compared to generalists, a lower number of countries in which they have a propensity to invest. Thus, specialists hold an internationally more specialized portfolio than generalists.

Moreover, the number of countries in which a private equity company has a propensity to invest depends on the number of industries in which the private equity company would invest as well as on whether it specializes in a particular industry (industries), but not on the number of stages in which the private equity company would invest nor on whether it specializes in firms' early stage of development. The higher the number of industries is, that is, the more industrially diversified the portfolio of a private equity company is, the lower the number of countries in the private equity companies' portfolios. Moreover, a high industrial specialization in private equity companies' portfolios results in a lower number of countries in the private equity companies' portfolios. These results suggest that private equity

Table 8.4 Characteristics of private equity companies
This table reports estimation results based on the VCPro dataset and on the German and French VC datasets. The funds under management are in millions of euros. A NEGBIN model is used when explaining the number of countries in which private equity companies have a propensity to invest. A LOGIT model is used when explaining a dummy variable which is equal to one if the private equity company indicated to invest internationally, and zero otherwise. Absolute z-statistics are given below the coefficients. *** (**, *) denotes significance at the 1 (5, 10) per cent level.

	(1)	(2)	(3)	(4)	(5)	(6)
	VCPro dataset				German dataset	French dataset
	NEGBIN		LOGIT		LOGIT	
Funds under management	0.000*** (4.25)	0.000*** (4.37)	0.002*** (3.46)	0.002*** (3.48)		
Specialists	–0.339*** (3.08)	–0.264** (2.52)	–0.509** (2.27)	–0.366* (1.66)		
Government	–0.623 (1.51)	–0.629 (1.57)	–2.362*** (2.79)	–2.170*** (2.85)		
Corporate company						–2.175** (2.55)
Savings-bank-based company					–1.615** (2.26)	
Independent company					0.331 (0.68)	–0.990* (1.75)
Number of industries	–0.023** (2.49)	–0.078*** (4.62)				
Number of stages	0.025 (0.82)	0.038 (0.52)				
Industrial specialization		0.243** (2.39)		0.871*** (3.86)	0.033 (0.07)	–0.516 (0.91)
Early-stage specialization		–0.172 (1.24)		–0.228 (0.87)	–0.849* (–1.89)	–1.178 (–1.46)
Constant	1.238 (1.42)	0.884 (1.04)	0.228 (0.26)	–0.922 (1.16)	–0.167 (0.46)	1.058** (2.45)
Number of observations	632	632	632	632	124	72
χ^2	94.96	91.53	89.713	94.853	10.287	11.081
Pseudo R^2	0.018	0.017	0.206	0.198	0.086	0.131

Source: VCPro dataset, German VC dataset, French VC dataset, own calculations.

companies aim at having either an internationally diversified and industrially specialized portfolio, or an internationally specialized and industrially diversified portfolio.

Estimation results for the dummy variable capturing internationalization based on the VCPro database are presented in columns (3) and (4) in Table 8.4. Internationalization of private equity companies depends on the volume of funds under management and on the type of the private equity company. The likelihood that a private equity company is internationally active increases with the volume of the private equity funds it manages. Moreover, the likelihood that a private equity company is internationally active is lower for specialists and for government-based companies than for generalists.

Whether a private equity company invests internationally also depends on the number of industries as well as on the industrial specialization but not on the number of stages nor on the early-stage specialization. The higher the number of industries is, or the higher the industrial specialization in private equity companies' portfolios is, the lower the probability that they would invest abroad. This finding is in line with the explanation for internationalization in private equity industries given above: since many European countries are relatively small, private equity companies must be either internationally active to be industrially specialized, which might be relevant to accumulate technological knowledge, or they must be industrially diversified to reach a sufficient deal flow.

Deeper insights into the role of the organizational structure of private equity companies can be gained from the German and French VC datasets. The organizational structure is likely to have an impact on the degree of internationalization because it is not equally beneficial for all private equity companies, since apart from aiming at obtaining high returns, they differ in their goals. Government-based private equity companies are interested in mitigating market failures (Gebhardt and Schmidt 2002, Lerner 2002a, European Commission 2000). Therefore, they are interested in investing in domestic firms. Bank-based private equity companies may be interested in investing equity capital in those firms in which they also hold debt claims. Only when the parent bank involved is internationally active, bank-based private equity companies are also expected to be internationally active. Savings-bank-based private equity companies are expected to have a strong focus on financing young firms located in their own geographic neighbourhood. By contrast, corporate private equity companies may have an interest in building long-term cooperative relationships and in keeping an eye on new technological developments (Riyanto and Schwienbacher 2002, Schween 1996). Therefore, they are less likely to have a geographical preference in their investments. Independent private equity companies may be internationalized more often especially in those countries with poor opportunities for raising new funds and with poor and limited investment opportunities.

I also created variables that measure the investment specialization of German and French private equity companies. In the German sample, I created a dummy variable for industrial specialization in the portfolios. This dummy variable is equal to one if a private equity company indicated to invest in less than eight industries of the total 23 industries distinguished, and zero otherwise. Thirty nine per cent of the 143 private equity companies indicated that they are industrially specialized. Moreover, I created a dummy variable for specialization in the early stage. This dummy variable equals one if a private equity company indicated that it would invest in the early stage and in not more than three stages of the total seven development stages distinguished, and zero otherwise. Thirteen per cent of the 143 private equity companies indicated that they are specialized in the early stage of firms' development.

In the French sample, the dummy variable for industrial specialization equals one if a private equity company indicated that it would invest in less than six industries of the total 15 industries distinguished, and zero otherwise. Twenty seven per cent of the 139 private equity companies indicated that they are industrially specialized. The dummy variable for early-stage specialization is equal to one if a private equity company indicated that it would invest in the early stage and in not more than one additional stage of the total five development stages distinguished, and zero otherwise. Sixteen per cent of the 139 private equity companies indicated that they are specialized in the early stage.

Columns (5) and (6) in Table 8.4 present estimation results based on the German and the French VC datasets. For the German sample, only savings-bank-based private equity companies turn out to have a lower likelihood being internationally active than either independent private equity companies or bank-based private equity companies. For the French sample, bank-based private equity companies turn out to have a higher likelihood than both independent and corporate private equity companies. In both datasets, industrial specialization does not matter as regards the likelihood of internationalization.

However, one interesting point to be reported is that early-stage specialization has a significantly negative impact on internationalization in the German sample. This is in line with the argument that early-stage investments require closer contacts between private equity companies and high-technology firms, which call for a geographically specialized portfolio.

To sum up, the three datasets that inform on the propensity of private equity companies to invest abroad offer some insights with regard to the link between internationalization and early-stage and industrial specialization. However, the links are not the same in all the datasets. Industrial specialization affects internationalization when using the VCPro dataset but not when using the French and German VC datasets.

Characteristics on a countrywide basis

Internationalization in private equity industries can also be analysed using the countrywide data from the EVCA statistics. I analysed these data in two steps. In the first step, I analysed whether the relevance of international investments is related to the relevance of different types of private equity companies on a countrywide basis. In the second step, I analysed whether the relevance of international investments can be explained by country-specific characteristics.

I analysed the relevance of different types of private equity companies for the international investments using the following empirical model:

$$\Delta IPE_{it} = X_{it}\beta + C_i + \varepsilon_{it} \tag{8.1}$$

where ΔIPE_{it} denotes either the percentage change in the volume or the number of international investments in country i at time t, X_{it} denotes the row vector of exogenous variables, C_i denotes the country-specific effects, and ε_{it} is the error term. Equation (8.1) was estimated using a fixed effects estimator. Table A5 presents the variables and sources used.

Table 8.5 gives the estimation results of the link between the percentage change in international investments and growth in investments by various types of private equity companies, that is, by dependent, semi-dependent, government-based and independent private equity companies. On a countrywide basis, I do not find a significant link between the percentage change in investments by dependent, semi-dependent, and government-based private equity companies. I find, however, that the percentage change in investments managed by independent private equity companies is significantly positive related to the percentage change in international investments. Thus, international private equity investments are likely to be managed more often by independent private equity companies. This result holds for the percentage change in the volume of international investments and the number of international investments. In addition, this result is not sensitive

Table 8.5 Growth in international investments
This table reports estimation results for internationalization in private equity industries. The endogenous variable is either the percentage change in the volume in international investments (investment volume) or in the number in international investments (investment number). Results are based on a fixed effects estimator including time dummies. ΔV denotes the percentage change in the volume of investments by various types of private equity companies. Δ*N* denotes the percentage change in the number of investments by various types of private equity companies. In columns (2) and (5), the United Kingdom is excluded from the sample. In columns (3) and (6), the years 1999 to 2002 are excluded from the sample. Absolute heteroscedasticity-consistent t-statistics are given below the coefficients. *** (**, *) denotes significance at the 1 (5, 10) per cent level.

	(1)	(2)	(3)	(4)	(5)	(6)
	Investment volume ΔV			Investment number ΔN		
Dependent	0.022	0.027	0.018	0.114	0.138	0.268
	(0.15)	(0.18)	(0.09)	(0.31)	(0.36)	(0.52)
Semi-dependent	0.052	0.046	0.135	0.131	0.141	0.606
	(0.62)	(0.52)	(1.08)	(0.41)	(0.42)	(1.19)
Government	–0.097	–0.103	–0.162	–0.333	–0.349	–0.559
	(1.15)	(1.17)	(1.28)	(1.27)	(1.27)	(1.36)
Independent	0.769***	0.779***	0.814***	2.264***	2.305***	3.266***
	(4.51)	(4.37)	(3.57)	(4.73)	(4.63)	(4.77)
Constant	–1.652	–1.828	–1.714	1.137	–0.951	0.268
	(1.36)	(1.39)	(1.15)	(0.93)	(0.77)	(0.2)
Number of observations	173	161	110	176	164	113
Number of countries	16	15	15	16	15	15

Source: EVCA (various issues), own calculations.

to the sample chosen. Neither excluding the United Kingdom (columns (2) and (5)) nor the years 1999 to 2002 (columns (3) and (6)) changes my estimation results significantly.

In the second step, I analysed the relevance of country-specific characteristics for internationalization by using the following empirical model:

$$IF_{it} = Y_{it}\lambda + C_i + \varepsilon_{it} \tag{8.2}$$

where IF_{it} denotes new funds raised internationally to new funds raised domestically in country i at time t, Y_{it} denotes the row vector of exogenous variables, C_i denotes the country-specific effects, and ε_{it} is the error term. Equation (8.2) was estimated using a fixed effects estimator.

The exogenous variables include the short-term interest rate and the GDP growth rate, in order to capture macroeconomic condi-

Table 8.6 The degree of internationalization in fund raising
This table reports estimation results for the degree of internationalization in fund raising. The dependent variable is new funds raised internationally to new funds raised domestically. The estimation method used is a country-fixed effects estimator; time dummies are included. In column (2), the United Kingdom is excluded from the sample. In column (3), the years 1999 to 2002 are excluded from the sample. Absolute heteroscedasticity-consistent t-statistics are given below the coefficients. *** (**, *) denotes significance at the 1 (5, 10) per cent level.

	(1)	(2)	(3)
Short-term interest rate	0.033	0.002	0.048
	(0.58)	(0.03)	(1.44)
Growth rate of GDP	1.306	1.657	0.073
	(0.54)	(0.67)	(0.07)
Capital gains tax rate	–0.045*	–0.044*	–0.036**
	(1.95)	(1.86)	(2.07)
Access to local capital markets	0.009	0.015	–0.004
	(0.22)	(0.34)	(0.27)
Constant	2.332***	2.314***	0.997
	(3.06)	(2.98)	(0.7)
Number of observations	163	152	99
Number of countries	16	15	16

Source: see Table A5, own calculations.

tions. Moreover, the exogenous variables include a measure of general investors' access to local capital markets, and the capital gains tax rates. I expected to find a positive coefficient of the GDP growth rate, which is likely to capture demand effects, a negative coefficient of the access to local capital markets (a high indicator means restricted access for foreign investors), and a negative impact of the capital gains tax rate, since higher capital gains taxes imply, *ceteris paribus*, lower investment incentives for foreign investors.

Table 8.6 reports the estimation results for the relationship between internationally raised funds and country-specific characteristics. Neither the short-term interest rate, nor the GDP growth rate, nor access to local capital markets help in explaining the share of funds raised abroad relative to the funds raised at home. However, the share of funds raised abroad depends significantly negative on the capital gains tax rate. Again, this result holds for a sub-sample from which the United Kingdom was excluded (column (2)) as well as for a sub-sample that covers only the years 1991 to 1998 (column (3)).

Summary

European private equity industries have become more internationalized in recent years. Private equity companies not only raise new funds abroad, but they also invest in foreign firms, although the control mechanisms used in venture capital finance can hardly be used over long distances. There are several explanations for this internationalization in private equity industries. These have, however, not been addressed in empirical research. First empirical results based on microdata indicate that the internationalization of private equity companies depends on the characteristics of private equity companies, such as industrial specialization and the type of the company. First empirical results based on countrywide data indicate that capital gains tax rates are significant driver of internationalization in fundraising.

9
Summary and Concluding Remarks

This book has two aims. The first aim was to paint a picture of the microeconomics of venture capital finance in Europe as colourfully as possible. To this end, fundraising, investing and exiting behaviours as well as portfolio specialization and internationalization strategies were discussed. The second aim was to describe and discuss various industry features of European venture capital and private equity industries. To this end, cross-country variations in venture capital and private equity investments, the link between the allocation of venture capital investments across industries and the development and creation of industries, and the link between internationalization in the venture capital industry and globalization in financial markets were discussed.

To understand the microeconomics of venture capital finance in Europe, the heterogeneity of private equity companies is important. Private equity companies differ with respect to their relationship to capital providers, such as pension funds and banks. In the case of a dependent private equity company that receives capital from banks, its managers are less likely to receive incentive-enhancing compensation than managers of independent private equity companies. Without incentive-enhancing compensation, managers neither participate directly in profits nor in the risks of the private equity investments.

This heterogeneity among private equity companies matters not only for the relationship to capital providers, but also for the relationship between private equity companies and their portfolio firms. More specifically, if managers of private equity companies do not receive incentive-enhancing compensation, they have lower incentives to push hard for their portfolio firms to perform well. Thus, the monitoring and management support services provided by managers without incentive-enhancing compensation are likely to be lower than the services provided by managers with incentive-enhancing compensation. This is likely to be reflected in the value that private equity companies add to their portfolio firms. Managers in private equity companies without incentive-enhancing compensation are less likely to add value to their portfolio firms than managers with incentive-enhancing compensation.

In addition, this heterogeneity among private equity companies matters for portfolio strategies. As compared to independent private equity companies, private equity companies that are dependent on their capital providers (except corporate private equity companies) are less likely to be specialized in particular industries, and they are less likely to finance the early stage of firms' development. A lower degree of industrial specialization might lead to lower experience in particular industries, which might result in a lower value that private equity companies add to the firms in their portfolios.

Moreover, this heterogeneity among private equity companies matters as regards exiting and the performance of private equity companies. While independent private equity companies aim at exiting from their portfolio firms after a certain time, dependent private equity companies might not have such goals, since they might be interested either in building up long-term corporate relationships or lending relationships. These additional goals of dependent private equity companies are likely to result in lower return demands when investing private equity than those of independent private equity companies.

The discussion of the literature dealing with the microeconomics of venture capital finance in Europe (Chapters 3, 4, 5, 8) indicated a need for future research. There is a need for future research because only few empirical studies have taken the heterogeneity among private equity companies into account, while other studies have failed to control for the heterogeneity among private equity companies. For example, some results of recent empirical studies with respect to the value that private equity companies add to the portfolio firms rest on the assumption of a homogenous group of private equity companies. Moreover, some studies have failed to control for the fact that private-equity-backed firms are a positively selected group that can only be compared with non-private-equity-backed firms after controlling for private equity companies' positive selection. In addition, there is a need for future research because research has not controlled for the cyclical behaviour in the private equity industries sufficiently. Controlling for industry cycle effects is important because the value that private equity companies add to their portfolio firms is likely to be more pronounced in times characterized by low private equity inflows than in times with large private equity inflows.

The discussion of the industry features showed that European countries differ substantially not only regarding private equity investments, but also regarding the allocation of private equity investments across various stages of portfolio firms' development. An empirical analysis showed that variations in private equity investments across European countries are explained by the design of financial markets, especially the development in stock markets for fast-growing firms, by entrepreneurial, tax and labour market regulations, and by the countries' human capital endowment. Macroeconomic developments such as short-term interest rates and growth in GDP did not substantially help in explaining variations in private equity investments across European countries.

Industrial structure and comparative advantages in the production of goods in Europe might be related to the industry features of private equity industries. Tentative results pointed to a positive relationship between private equity investments and comparative advantages for selected industries in which European private equity companies prefer to invest. Generally, however, the role that private equity companies play in the creation of new industries and in changing the face of existing industries has received little attention in the literature. Additional research is warranted to deepen our understanding of the role of private equity finance in transforming industries and countries' comparative advantages.

An additional research field that is relatively unexplored is internationalization in private equity industries. Substantial amounts of private equity funds and investments have flowed across countries in recent years. This internationalization is to some extent astonishing because the monitoring and management support services provided by particular private equity companies are in line with regionally segmented capital markets. On a countrywide basis, the degree of internationalization in private equity investments depends on the heterogeneity of private equity companies; an industry characterized by many independent private equity companies has a higher degree of internationalization in investments than an industry characterized by many dependent private equity companies. However, the degree of internationalization in private equity funds does not seem to depend on macroeconomic conditions except as regards the capital gains tax rates. Here, additional research is warranted to deepen our understanding of the role of internationalization for private equity companies and for the development of private equity industries in other countries.

In order to give a brief overview of the European private equity industries under consideration, Table 9.1 summarizes the main characteristics discussed throughout the book. Some countries have been successful in establishing private equity industries. The private equity industry in the United Kingdom not only has a high EVCA score of the tax and legal

Table 9.1 Summary of private equity industries in Europe
This table summarizes the characteristics of private equity industries in Europe.

(1) shows the EVCA score on the tax and legal environment. X (XX, XXX) means that the tax and legal environment is not favourable (neutral, favourable) for private equity finance. See discussion in Chapter 2.

(2) shows the size of new funds raised relative to GDP in 2003: X<1.0, 1.0≤XX≤4.0, XXX>4.0. See discussion in Chapter 2.

(3) provides information on the role of independent private equity companies. X means independent venture capital companies invested less than 40 per cent of the private equity investments: X<40, 40≤XX≤60, 60≤XXX≤80, and XXXX≥80. See discussion in Chapter 3.

(4) offers information on the role of governments as a source of new funds. X means more than 15 per cent of the new funds come from governments: X>15, 10≤XX≤15, 5≤XXX≤10, and XXXX≥5. See discussion in Chapter 3.

(5) gives the size of private equity investments relative to GDP in 2003: X<1.0, 1.0≤XX≤4.0, XXX>4.0. See discussion in Chapter 2.

(6) provides information on the importance of early-stage investments relative to private-equity investments. X means less than 10 per cent of the private equity are invested in the early stage of development: X<10, 10≤XX≤20, 20≤XXX≤30, and XXXX≥30. See discussion in Chapter 4.

(7) gives an overview on the concentration of investments on firms operating in the IT and BIO industry. X means less than 40 per cent of the private equity are invested in firms operating in the IT or BIO industry: X<40, 40≤XX≤50, 50≤XXX≤60, and XXXX≥60. See discussion in Chapter 4.

(8) provides information on the comparative advantages in those industries in which private equity companies prefer to invest. The first number informs on the number of industries in which the country has a comparative advantage; the second number informs on the number of industries distinguished in the empirical analysis. See discussion in Chapter 7.

(9) shows the percentage of internationally raised funds. X means internationally internationally raised new funds account for less than 10 per cent of the total new funds raised: X<10, 10≤XX≤20, 20≤XXX≤30, and XXXX≥30. See discussion in Chapter 8.

Table 9.1 Summary of private equity industries in Europe – *continued*
This table summarizes the characteristics of private equity industries in Europe.

	(1) EVCA score	(2) New funds raised	(3) Independent companies	(4) Governments	(5) Private equity investments	(6) Early-stage focus	(7) Technology focus	(8) Comparative advantages	(9) International raised funds
Austria	X	X	XXX	X	X	XXX	XXX	0/7	XXX
Belgium	XX	X	X	XXX	XX	XXX	XXX	4/7	XX
Denmark	X	XX	XXXX	XXX	XX	XXX	XXX	3/7	XX
Finland	X	XX	XX	XX	XX	XXXX	XXX	4/7	X
France	XX	XX	XX	XXX	XX	XX	X	4/7	XXX
Germany	X	X	XX	XXX	XX	XX	X	4/7	XXX
Greece	XX	X	XX	XXX	X	XXX	X	0/7	na
Ireland	XXX	X	XX	XX	XX	XXX	XXXX	na	XX
Italy	XX	XX	X	XXXX	XX	XX	X	1/7	XXX
Netherlands	XX	XXX	XX	XXXX	XX	XX	X	4/7	X
Norway	XX	XX	XXX	XXX	XX	XX	XXX	2/7	X
Portugal	XX	X	X	X	X	XX	X	0/6	X
Spain	XX	XX	XXX	XX	XX	XX	X	0/7	XXXX
Sweden	XX	XXX	XXX	XXX	XX	X	X	3/6	XXX
Switzerland	XX	XX	XXX	XXXX	XX	XX	XX	na	XX
United Kingdom	XXX	XXX	XXX	XXXX	XXX	X	X	4/7	XXXX

environment, but is also characterized by a relatively high degree of independent private equity companies, a relatively low degree of government influence, and a high degree of internationalization. However, the private equity industry in the United Kingdom shows a lower degree of specialization in the early stage and in particular industries than in other European countries.

In strong contrast to the private equity industry in the United Kingdom, the private equity industries in Austria and Greece are hardly existent. Austria has a very bad EVCA score of the tax and legal environment for the private equity industry, while Greece has a somewhat better EVCA score. The private equity industries in these two countries also differ with respect to independent private equity companies and with respect to the role of governments as capital providers. However, in both countries, private equity is invested intensively in firms that are in the early stage of development, and both countries have no comparative advantage in industries preferred by private equity companies.

Overall Table 9.1 summarizes the existing heterogeneity and also the complexity of the private equity industries for European countries. It cannot be expected that either the heterogeneity or the complexity of these industries will be significantly reduced in the future. Particular sources of heterogeneity in these industries, such as pension funds as capital providers, might change in the future because of softened regulations. However, since private equity finance, and especially venture capital finance, is a highly specialized form of finance, one should not expect that such industries will develop similarly in all countries.

Appendices

Table A1 Datasets used in this book

EVCA statistics (www.evca.com)
The European Venture Capital Association (EVCA) reports annual data on aggregated private equity investments and sources of new funds raised for private equity investments. With respect to investment data, the EVCA data are broken down according to types of private equity companies, syndicated and non-syndicated deals, foreign and domestic portfolio firms, development stages of portfolio firms and industries in which portfolio firms operate. With respect to new funds, the EVCA data are broken down according to various fund providers such as pension funds, insurance companies and banks. The EVCA provides data on more than 20 Western and Eastern European countries. In this book, however, I concentrated only on those Western European countries for which relatively long time series are available.
VCPro dataset (www.vcprodatabase.com)
This qualitative dataset informs on almost 800 European private equity companies. It provides information on the country of origin, the volume of funds under management, the type of the private equity company, its founding year, the minimum and maximum amount of single investments, industries and stages of firms' development and the geographic areas in which the companies would invest.
German VC dataset (www.bvk-ev.de)
The German VC dataset informs on characteristics of private equity companies provided by the Bundesverband Deutscher Kapitalgesellschaften (BVK). Specifically, it informs on the number of firms in private equity and their investment behaviour and gives qualitative data on fund providers. In order to identify the various types of private equity companies acting in the German market, I used information from the webpage of the BVK as well as from webpages of individual private equity companies. On the webpage of the BVK, private equity companies indicate who their shareholders are. This information was used to identify private equity companies that are bank-dependent. Private equity companies indicate on the BVK webpage whether they are profit-oriented. All non-profit oriented companies were classified as government-based companies. For all remaining private equity companies, I collected additional information from individual webpages.

Table A1 Datasets used in this book – *continued*

French VC dataset (www.afic.asso.fr)
The French VC dataset informs on characteristics of private equity companies provided by the Association Francaise des Investisseurs en Capital (AFIC) and Hugot (2000). Specifically, I have information on the number of portfolio firms, size of funds under management, and investment preferences. In order to identify the types of private equity companies acting in the French market, I also used information provided on the webpages of particular private equity companies if necessary. The member list of AFIC includes information on the legal status of the particular members. Combining the two sources, it was possible to identify all independent companies and most of the other types of private equity companies. Hugot (2000) contains information on the shareholders of private equity companies that I predominantly used to identify the bank-dependent companies.
IPO dataset on the German Neuer Markt and the French Nouveau Marché
The IPO dataset on the German Neuer Markt and the French Nouveau Marché was compiled by the project *European Financial Markets, Venture Capital and High-Tech Firms,* which was funded under the 5th framework of the European Commission (Contract No. HPSE–CT–1999–00039). This dataset includes firms that went public on the Neuer Markt between 1997 and 2000 and on the Nouveau Marché between 1996 and 2000. The Institut für Entscheidungstheorie und Unternehmensforschung (Karlsruhe), provided share prices of firms that went public on the Neuer Markt. The Bourse de Paris provided share prices of firms listed on the Nouveau Marché as well as the offer prices, gross proceeds, offer price ranges, number of shares sold and the underwriters of the firms that went public on the Nouveau Marché. Firm-specific data, such as private equity-backing, were collected from the Internet pages of the firms, from their annual reports and from their IPO prospectuses.

Table A2 Data definitions in the micro-datasets

Variables	Description
	VCPro dataset
Type of private equity company	Three types are distinguished: generalists, specialists and government.
Funds under management	Denotes the volume of funds under management in millions of euros.
Average investment volume	It is calculated from the minimum and maximum amounts that the private equity company intends to invest.
Number of industries	The number is between one and 18. The following industries are distinguished: aerospace and defence,

Table A2 Data definitions in the micro-datasets – *continued*

Variables	Description
	VCPro dataset
	agriculture and fishery, biotechnology, business products and services, chemicals and materials, communications and networking, computers and peripherals, consumer products and services, distribution/retailing, electronics, energy and natural resources, environment, financial services, food services and products, healthcare services, industrial products and services, internet technology, IT services, manufacturing, media and entertainment, medical devices and equipment, pharmaceuticals, real estate and construction, software, semiconductors, telecommunications, transportation, education and training.
Number of stages	The number is between one and 12. The following stages are distinguished: acquisition, consolidation, distressed debt, divestiture, expansion, going private, MBO/LBO, mezzanine, other early stages, PIPE, privatization, recapitalization, secondary purchase, seed, special situations, spinout, start-up, turnaround.
Industrial specialization	Dummy variable equals one if the private equity company indicated to invest in less than six industries, and zero otherwise.
Early-stage specialization	Dummy variable equals one if the private equity company indicated to invest solely in the seed, start-up, or other early stages, and zero otherwise.
	German VC dataset
Type of private equity company	Five types are distinguished: government-based, bank-based, savings-bank-based, corporate and independent private equity company.
Industrial specialization	Dummy variable equals one if the number of industries in which the private equity company would invest is less than seven, and zero otherwise.
Early-stage specialization	Dummy variable equals one if the number of stages in which the private equity company would invest is less than four stages, and indicated it would invest in the seed or start-up stage.
	French VC dataset
Type of private equity company	Four types are distinguished: bank-based, corporate, insurance-dependent and independent private equity companies.
Industrial specialization	Dummy variable equals one if the number of industries in which the private equity company indicated that it would invest is less than five, and zero otherwise.

Table A2 Data definitions in the micro-datasets – *continued*

Variables	Description
	French VC dataset
Early-stage specialization	Dummy variable equals one if the number of stages is less than three and if the private equity company indicated that it would invest in the start-up stage, and zero otherwise.

Table A3 Data definitions and sources Chapter 6

Variables	Description	Source
Endogenous variables	• Percentage change in early-stage investments. • Percentage change in early- and expansion-stage investments. • Percentage change in private equity investments. • Data coverage: 1991 to 2001. • Countries included: Austria, Belgium, Denmark, Finland, France, Greece, Germany, Ireland, Italy, the Netherlands, Norway, Portugal, Spain, Sweden, Switzerland, and the United Kingdom.	EVCA (various issues).
	Style of financial intermediation and financial markets	
New funds by pension funds	New funds provided by pension funds as a percentage of total new funds raised for private equity investments.	EVCA (various issues).
Bank assets to listed firms	Captures overall importance of banks as compared to organized financial markets.	OECD (2003b), Emerging stock markets factbook (1993, 2001)
Stock market returns	Annual returns on stock markets for fast-growing firms calculated from daily share indexes returns.	Datastream.
Stock market return volatility	Calculated from daily returns based on share indexes of stock markets for fast-growing firms.	Datastream.
Growth rate of new funds	Growth rate of new funds raised for private investments.	EVCA (various issues).
	Governments	
New funds by governments	New funds provided by governments as a percentage of total new funds raised for private equity investments.	EVCA (various issues).

Table A3 Data definitions and sources Chapter 6 – *continued*

Variables	Description	Source
	Tax and legal legislation	
Capital gains tax rate	for individuals.	Corporate tax guide (various issues).
Law tradition	Dummy equals one if the country has a common-law tradition or a civil-law tradition, and zero otherwise.	La Porta *et al.* (2000).
Anti-director rights	The index ranges from zero to five. Higher values mean higher shareholder protection.	La Porta *et al.* (2000).
Accounting standards	The International Accounting and Auditing Trends has created this index by examining how many of 90 accounting items were included in the 1990 annual reports of firms. Higher values mean better accounting standards.	La Porta *et al.* (2000).
	Entrepreneurial environment	
Growth rate of patents	Growth in the number of patent applications to the European patent office.	(OECD 2003c).
Labour index	Strictness of protection against dismissals of regular and temporary employment. Two values are available over the observation period. The value of the late 1980s is used for the years 1991–93, while the value of the late 1990s is used for the years 1994–2001.	OECD (1999), Table 2.5.
Survey indicators	• Firm creation: the higher the index is, the more the creation of firms is supported by legislation. • Entrepreneurship: the higher the index is, the more entrepreneurship of managers is widespread in the country.	IMD (various issues).
	Macroeconomic factors	
Short-term interest rate		IMF (2003).
Growth rate of GDP		OECD (2004).

Table A4 Data definitions and sources Chapter 7

Variables	Description	Source
Endogenous variables	Seven industries are distinguished: (1) the IT industry, (2) the BIO industry, (3) the ENERGY industry, (4) the AGRICULTURE industry, (5) the TRANSPORTATION industry, (6) the CHEMICAL industry, (7) and the IA industry. For each country *i* and each of these industries *j*, the following endogenous variable has been calculated: $r_{ijt} = Q_{ijt} / (Q_{ijt} - X_{ijt} + M_{ijt})$. The IT industry contains office, accounting and computing machinery (pr0130) and electrical machinery and apparatus (pr0131) and radio, television and communication equipment (pr0132). (2) The BIO industry contains pharmaceuticals (pr012423). (3) The ENERGY industry contains coke, refined petroleum products and nuclear fuel (pr0123) and mining and quarrying of energy-producing materials (pr011012). (4) The AGRICULTURE industry contains agriculture, hunting, forestry, fishing (pr010105) and wood and products of wood and cork (pr0120) and food products, beverages and tobacco (pr011516). (5) The TRANSPORTATION industry contains transport equipment (pr013435) and machinery and equipment (pr0129). (6) The CHEMICAL industry contains chemicals excluding pharmaceuticals (pr0124ex) and rubber and plastics products (pr0125). (7) The IA industry contains medical, precision and optical instruments, watches and clocks (pr0133). The following countries are included in the regression analysis: Austria, Belgium, Denmark, Finland, France, Greece, Germany, Italy, the Netherlands, Norway, Portugal, Spain, Sweden, and the United Kingdom.	OECD STAN database (various issues).

Table A4 Data definitions and sources Chapter 7 – *continued*

Variables	Description	Source
Private equity investments	Percentage change in private equity investments.	EVCA (various issues).
Bank assets	Percentage change in bank assets in order to capture endowment with bank capital.	OECD (2003b).
Stock market capitalization	Percentage change in stock market capitalization in order to capture endowment of equity capital.	Emerging stock market factbook (1996), (2004).
Research employees	Percentage change in business and government-research employees in order to capture human capital endowment.	OECD (2003c).

Table A5 Data definitions and sources Chapter 8

Variables	Description	Source
Endogenous variables	Table 8.5: percentage change in the volume or number in international investments. Table 8.6: new funds raised internationally to new funds raised domestically.	EVCA (various issues).
Type of VC company	Type is captured by the percentage change in the volume or number of investments undertaken by the particular type of private equity company. Four types of private equity companies are distinguished: independent, dependent, semi-dependent, and government-based private equity companies.	EVCA (various issues).
Short-term interest rate		IMF (2003).
Growth rate of GDP		OECD (2004).
Capital gains tax rate		Corporate tax guide (various issues).
Access to local capital markets	This measure is based on survey evidence on the ease of access to local capital markets for foreign investors. A high value of this variable means that foreign companies do not face restrictions in accessing the local capital market.	IMD (various issues).

Notes

1 For a comparison of European private equity industries and the US industry see Schertler (2002/2003).
2 www.evca.com
3 For the historical development of the German private equity industry with particular reference to the MBGs, see Pfirrmann *et al.* (1997).
4 www.siemensventurecapital.com
5 www.basf-vc.de
6 In Germany, private equity companies are usually legally constituted as a Kommanditgesellschaft. A management company is then the Komplementär (general partner), while capital providers are Kommanditisten (limited partners).
7 In dependent and semi-dependent private equity companies, professional managers often do not receive profit participation in addition to their basic salary. As a consequence, the incentives of these managers to support the management teams of the portfolio firms and to monitor the development of the firms in which they invest are different from the incentives of their independent counterparts (Zemke 1995).
8 Apart from returning cash to their capital providers, US venture capital companies distribute shares they hold in portfolio firms to their capital providers (Gompers and Lerner 1998). The distribution of shares in Europe has not been at the focus of academic research.
9 The dataset comprises 1,874 investment deals from the United States, 395 from France, 316 from the United Kingdom and 194 from Germany. The study has also indicated that periodic cashflow requirements are strongly affected by country-specific legality conditions; the probability of a periodic cashflow decreases by almost 2 per cent when the legality index improves from 20 to 21 for developed nations.
10 Bottazzi *et al.* (2004b) have mentioned several other contingent control clauses. In particular, in 54 per cent of the cases, private equity companies have the right to force a trade sale. In 36 per cent of the cases, private equity companies have rights to board control. In 31 per cent of the cases, they have the right to fire the chief executive officer.
11 Bergemann and Hege (1998) ascribe the staging of the capital infusion to unknown time profiles of future investment needs; the staging of capital infusions has an option value in their model because the capital invested is ultimately sunk.
12 In Germany, portfolio firms organized as private limited companies are not allowed to use convertible debt, while portfolio firms organized as public corporations are allowed to use equity and convertible securities (Bascha and Walz 2002b). Loans and proprietors' loans, as well as silent partnerships, are independent of the legal form of the portfolio firm. According to the study by Bascha and Walz (2002b), the silent partnerships are widely

used in the German private equity industry. However, a large number of private equity companies do not use silent partnerships at all.

13 The Small Business Investment Company (SBIC) programme, which was introduced in 1958, stimulated the establishment of small privately owned and managed investment companies. The Small Business Administration (SBA) provided SBICs four dollars for each dollar invested (Pfirrmann *et al.* 1997). SBICs dominated the US market for venture capital in the mid-1960s. Nearly 700 SBICs were licensed at that time (Bygrave and Timmons 1992).

14 The correlation between the dummy variable that is equal to one for specialists and the number of stages or the early-stage specialization of private equity companies is significant but the size of the correlation coefficient is rather low. Thus, the definition of specialists does not depend only on the early-stage specialization.

15 Since I did not control for endogeneity of the funds under management, coefficients do not inform on causality.

16 This argument predicts a positive relationship between syndication and investment returns. By contrast, Brander *et al.* (2002) have argued in favour of a negative relationship. At one extreme, if a business proposal is very promising and offers high expected returns, private equity companies will accept a proposal without the consultation of a second private equity company. Established private equity companies are likely to have the financial resources to finance portfolio firms without the help of a syndicate and try as a single investor to get all the financial benefits it can from a lucrative portfolio firm. At the other extreme, if they determine that a proposal is not of sufficient quality and potential, they will reject it without further consideration. Therefore, stand-alone investments should promise on average higher returns than syndicated investments.

17 For studies that analyse syndication of venture capital investments in the United States, see Bygrave (1987), Lerner (1994a) and Sorenson and Stuart (2002).

18 Exiting *via* stock markets does not have to take place *via* the national stock market, as the going public and listings of Israeli and Dutch firms on the NASDAQ indicate (Rock 2001, 2002, Blass and Yafeh 2001).

19 In Germany, the 4th Finanzmarktförderungsgesetz was passed in 2002. It aimed at introducing more flexibility, higher transparency and more stringent rules on insider trading by changing the Exchange Act (Börsengesetz) and the Securities Trading Act (Wertpapierhandelsgesetz) (Theissen 2003).

20 http://www.mackewicz.de

21 The IRR is defined as the discounting rate for which the present value of all future outflows equals the present value of all future inflows that a private equity fund generates over time. Several measurement problems occur when calculating the IRR. For example, as long as the capital of the private equity funds is still being invested, future flows of capital have to be estimated in order to calculate the IRR.

22 For example, it would be interesting to check whether the coefficients of small and large countries are similar in size. The size of a country may have implications for the size of the coefficients, since large countries may be more efficient in realizing economies of scale. Private equity companies

operating in large countries may realize economies of scale more often, since they may have more opportunities to syndicate their investments and to concentrate their investment activity on particular industries and stages of firms' development. Economies of scale may be reflected in lower coefficients of, for example, the human capital variable. Moreover, in the second half of the 1990s, the large countries in my sample developed comparatively liquid stock market segments for fast-growing firms, while the small countries failed to do so (Bottazzi and Da Rin 2002a, Tejada 2003a). However, distinguishing between small and large countries in this dynamic panel approach is not possible.

23 Information in EVCA statistics on the internationalization of private equity investments is limited. As Table 8.3 indicates, private equity inflows in this dataset are not international inflows but inflows from other European countries.

References

A. R. Admati and P. Pfleiderer, 'Robust Financial Contracting and the Role of Venture Capitalists', *Journal of Finance* 49 (1994) 371–402.

A. G. Ahearne, E. L. Griever and F. E. Warnock, 'Information Costs and Home Bias: An Analysis of US Holdings of Foreign Equities', *Journal of International Economics* 62 (2004) 313–36.

G. A. Akerlof, 'The Market for "Lemons": Quality Uncertainty and the Market Mechanism', *Quarterly Journal of Economics* 84 (1970) 488–500.

R. Amit, J. Brander and C. Zott, 'Why Do Venture Capital Firms Exist? Theory and Canadian Evidence', *Journal of Business Venturing* 13 (1998) 441–66.

R. Amit, L. Glosten and E. Muller, 'Entrepreneurial Ability, Venture Investments, and Risk Sharing', *Management Science* 36 (1990) 1232–45.

T. W. Anderson and C. Hsiao, 'Formulation and Estimation of Dynamic Models Using Panel Data', *Annals of Applied Econometrics* 1 (1982) 47–82.

AVCJ (Asian Venture Capital Journal), 'The 2005 Guide to Venture Capital in Asia', www.asianfn.com (2005).

D. B. Audretsch and E. Lehmann, 'Debt or Equity? The Role of Venture Capital in Financing the New Economy in Germany', Discussion Paper 3656, Centre of Economic Policy Research (CEPR) (2002).

M. Baker and P. A. Gompers, 'An Analysis of Executive Compensation, Ownership, and Control in Closely Held Firms', Working Paper, Harvard Business School, Boston, MA (1999).

B. Balassa, 'Comparative Advantages in Manufactured Goods: A Reappraisal', *Review of Economics and Statistics* 68 (1986) 315–19.

R. Baldwin, 'Exporting the Capital Markets: Comparative Advantage and Capital Market Imperfections', in D. Audretsch, L. Sleuwaegen and H. Yamawaki (eds), *The Convergence of International and Domestic Markets*, Amsterdam: North-Holland (1989).

D. Barlow and M. Robson, 'Have Unincorporated Businesses in the UK been Constrained in their Ability to Obtain Bank Lending?', *Applied Financial Economics* 12 (2002) 673–80.

E. Barnes and Y. McCarthy, 'Grandstanding in the UK Venture Capital Industry', EFMA 2002 London Meetings (2002).

J. M. Barron and N. T. Valev, 'International Lending by U.S. Banks', *Journal of Money, Credit and Banking* 32 (2000) 357–81.

C. B. Barry, 'New Directions in Research on Venture Capital Finance', *Journal of the Financial Management Association* 23 (1994) 3–15.

C. B. Barry, C. J. Muscarella, J. W. Peavy III and M. R. Vetsuypens, 'The Role of Venture Capital in the Creation of Public Companies: Evidence from the Going-Public Process', *Journal of Financial Economics* 27 (1990) 447–71.

A. Bascha and U. Walz, 'Convertible Securities and Optimal Exit Decisions in Venture Capital Finance', *Journal of Corporate Finance* 7 (2002a) 285–306.

A. Bascha and U. Walz, 'Financing Practices in the German Venture Capital Industry: An Empirical Assessment', Working Paper 08, Center for Financial Studies (CFS) (2002b).

G. Baygan, 'Venture Capital Policy Review: United Kingdom', STI Working Paper 1, Industry Issues, Organization for Economic Co-operation and Development (OECD) (2003a).

G. Baygan, 'Venture Capital Policy Review: Norway', STI Working Paper 17, Industry Issues, Organization for Economic Co-operation and Development (OECD) (2003b).

G. Baygan, 'Venture Capital Policy Review: Sweden', STI Working Paper 11, Industry Issues, Organization for Economic Co-operation and Development (OECD) (2003c).

G. Baygan and M. Freudenberg, 'The Internationalisation of Venture Capital Activity in OECD Countries: Implications for Measurement and Policy', STI Working Papers 7, Organization for Economic Co-operation and Development (OECD), Paris (2000).

T. Beck and R. Levine, 'Industry Growth and Capital Allocation: Does Having a Market- or Bank-Based System Matter?', Working Paper 8982, National Bureau of Economic Research (NBER) (2002).

D. Bergemann and U. Hege, 'Venture Capital Financing, Moral Hazard, and Learning', *Journal of Banking & Finance* 22 (1998) 703–35.

G. Bernile, D. Cumming and E. Lyandres, 'The Size of Venture Capitalists Portfolios', RICAFE 018, London School of Economics and Political Science (2005).

Berwin & Co, 'Venture Capital Incentives in Europe: Outlines Fiscal and Legal Incentives Specifically Relating to Venture Investing in 10 European Countries', accessed on September 18, 2001, at http://www.evca.com/publications.html (1997).

C. Beuselinck, M. Deloof and S. Manigart, 'Venture Capital, Private Equity and Earnings Quality', Working Paper 221, Ghent University (2004).

K. Bingham, N. Ferguson and J. Lerner, 'Schröder Ventures: Launch of the Euro Fund', HBS case 9–297–026, Harvard Business School, Boston, MA (1998).

J. R. Birkinshaw, R. B. Batenburg and G. Murray, 'Corporate Venturing: The State of the Art and the Prospects for the Future', Working Paper, London School of Economics and Political Science (2002).

B. S. Black and R. J. Gilson, 'Venture Capital and the Structure of Capital Markets: Banks versus Stock Markets', *Journal of Financial Economics* 47 (1998) 243–77.

A. Blass and Y. Yafeh, 'Vagabond Shoes Longing to Stray: Why Foreign Firms List in the United States', *Journal of Banking and Finance* 25 (2001) 555–72.

R. Blundell and S. Bond, 'Initial Conditions and Moment Restrictions in Dynamic Panel Data Models', *Journal of Econometrics* 87 (1998) 115–43.

R. Blundell, R. Griffith and J. Van Reenen, 'Dynamic Count Data Models of Technological Innovation', *Economic Journal* 105 (1995) 333–44.

S. Bond, D. Harhoff and J. Van Reenen, 'Investment, R&D and Financial Constraints in Britain and Germany', Working Paper Series 5, The Institute for Fiscal Studies (1999).

L. Bottazzi and M. Da Rin, 'Venture Capital in Europe and the Financing of Innovative Companies', *Economic Policy* 34 (2002a) 231–69.

L. Bottazzi and M. Da Rin, 'Europe's New Stock Markets', Discussion Paper 3521, Centre of Economic Policy Research (CEPR) (2002b).

L. Bottazzi, M. Da Rin and T. Hellmann, 'Active Financial Intermediation: Evidence on the Role of Organizational Specialization and Human Capital', Working Paper 266, Innozenzo Gasparini Institute for Economic Research (IGIER) (2004a).

L. Bottazzi, M. Da Rin and T. Hellmann, 'The Changing Face of the European Venture Capital Industry: Facts and Analysis', *The Journal of Private Equity* 7 (2004b) 26–53.

L. Bottazzi, M. Da Rin and T. Hellmann, 'What Role of Legal Systems in Financial Intermediation? Theory and Evidence', RICAFE 022, London School of Economics and Political Science (2005).

R. Bouis, 'IPOs Cycle and Investment in High-Tech Industries', Working Paper 47, Center for Financial Studies (CFS) (2003).

J. A. Brander, R. Amit and W. Antweiler, 'Venture-Capital Syndication: Improved Venture Selection vs. the Value-Added Hypothesis', *Journal of Economics and Management Strategy* 11 (2002) 423–52.

A. Brav and P. Gompers, 'Myth or Reality? The Long-Run Underperformance of Initial Public Offerings: Evidence from Venture and Non Venture Capital-Backed Companies', *The Journal of Finance* 52 (1997) 1791–821.

M. Brouwer and B. Hendrix, 'Two Worlds of Venture Capital: What Happened to US and Dutch Early Stage Investment?', *Small Business Economics* 10 (1998) 333–48.

O. Bürgel, A. Fier, G. Licht and G. Murray, 'Internationalisation of High-Tech Start-ups and Fast Growth-Evidence for UK and Germany', Discussion Paper 00–35, Zentrum für Europäische Wirtschaftsforschung GmbH (ZEW) (2000).

BVK (Bundesverband Deutscher Kapitalbeteiligungsgesellschaften), BVK-Statistik, Berlin, (various issues).

W. D. Bygrave, 'Syndicated Investments by Venture Capital Firms: A Networking Perspective', *Journal of Business Venturing* 2 (1987) 139–54.

W. D. Bygrave and J. A. Timmons, *Venture Capital at the Crossroads*, Boston, MA: Harvard Business School Press (1992).

A. C. Cameron and P. K. Trivedi, 'Econometric Models Based on Count Data: Comparisons and Applications of Some Estimators and Tests', *Journal of Applied Econometrics* 1 (1986) 29–53.

C. Casamatta, 'Financing and Advising: Optimal Financial Contracts with Venture Capitalists', *The Journal of Finance* 58 (2003) 2059–85.

C. E. Christensen and J. L. Christensen, 'The Impact of Venture Capital in Denmark', in M. v. Zedtwitz, G. Haour, T. M. Khalil and L. A. Lefebvre (eds), *Management of Technology: Growth through Business Innovation and Entrepreneurship*, Amsterdam: Pergamon (2003).

F. Cornelli and O. Yosha, 'Stage Financing and the Role of Convertible Securities', *The Review of Economic Studies* 70 (2003) 1–32.

Corporate tax guide, New York: Ernst and Young (various issues).

D. Cumming, D. Schmidt and U. Walz, 'Legality and Venture Governance around the World', Working Paper 010, Innozenzo Gasparini Institute for Economic Research (IGIER) (2004).

D. Cumming and U. Walz, 'Private Equity Returns and Disclosure around the World', RICAFE 009, London School of Economics and Political Science (2004).

M. Da Rin, G. Nicodano and A. Sembenelli, 'Public Policy and the Creation of Active Venture Capital Markets', Working Paper 270, Innozenzo Gasparini Institute for Economic Research (IGIER) (2004).

D. Dahl and R. E. Shrieves, 'The Extension of International Credit by US Banks: A Disaggregated Analysis, 1988–1994', *Journal of International Money and Finance* 18 (1999) 153–67.

D. De Clercq and D. P. Dimov, 'Explaining Venture Capital Firms' Syndicate Behavior: A Longitudinal Study', Working Paper 279, Ghent University (2004).

D. De Clercq and H. J. Sapienza, 'When Do Venture Capital Firms Learn from Their Portfolio Companies?', Working Paper 222, Ghent University (2004).

G. De la Dehesa, 'Venture Capital in the United States and Europe', Occasional Paper 65, Group of Thirty, Washington, DC (2002).

D. De Meza, 'Overlending?', *The Economic Journal* 112 (2002) F17–F31.

A. Demigüc-Kunt and V. Maksimovic, 'Law, Finance, and Firm Growth', *Journal of Finance* 53 (1998) 2107–37.

C. Diller and C. Kaserer, 'What Drives Cash Flow Based European Private Equity Returns? – Fund Inflows, Skilled GPs and/or Risk?', RICAFE 015, London School of Economics and Political Science (2005).

D. Dohse, 'Technology Policy and the Regions – The Case of the BioRegio Contest', *Research Policy* 29 (2000) 1111–33.

D. Dohse and A. Schertler, 'Explaining the Regional Distribution of New Economy Firms – A Count Data Analysis', Working Paper 1193, Kiel Institute for World Economics (2004).

J. A. Doukas and H. Gonenc, 'Long-Term Performance of New Equity Issuers, Venture Capital and Reputation of Investment Bankers', Working Paper, SSRN (2001).

EBAN (European Business Angel Network), 'Dissemination Report on the Potential for Business Angels Investments and Networks in Europe' (1998).

J. Egeln, G. Licht and F. Steil, 'Firm Foundations and the Role of Financial Constraints', *Small Business Economics* 9 (1997) 137–50.

B. Elango, V. H. Fried, R. D. Hisrich and A. Polonchek, 'How Venture Capital Firms Differ', *Journal of Business Venturing* 10 (1995) 157–79.

Emerging stock market factbook, New York: International Finance Corporation (IFC) (various issues).

D. Engel, 'Welche Regionen profitieren von Venture Capital Aktivitäten?', Discussion Paper 02–37, Zentrum für Europäische Wirtschaftsforschung GmbH (ZEW) (2002).

D. Engel, 'Venture Capital für junge Unternehmen', Nomos Verlag, Schriftreihe des ZEW: Band 71, Zentrum für Europäische Wirtschaftsforschung GmbH (ZEW) (2003a).

D. Engel, 'Höheres Beschäftigungswachstum durch Venture Capital?', *Journal of Economics and Statistics* 223 (2003b) 1–22.

D. Engel and M. Keilbach, 'Firm Level Implications of Early Stage Venture Capital Investments – An Empirical Investigation', Discussion Paper 02–82, Zentrum für Europäische Wirtschaftsforschung GmbH (ZEW) (2002).

European Commission, 'Progress Report on the Risk Capital Action Plan', Communication from the Commission to the Council and the European Parliament, Brussels, COM (2000) 658 final.

EVCA (European Venture Capital Association), Yearbook, Zaventem, Belgium (1991–2003).
EVCA (European Venture Capital Association), 'Pan-European Survey of Performance', ENN Supplement, October 2001. Accessed on March 6, 2002, at http://www.evca.com/publications.html (2001a).
EVCA (European Venture Capital Association), 'Pan-European Survey of Performance', ENN Supplement, October 2002. Access on December 18, 2002, at http://www.evca.com/publications.html (2002a).
EVCA (European Venture Capital Association), 'Performance Measurement and Asset Allocation for European Private Equity Funds', Research Paper (2004a).
EVCA (European Venture Capital Association), 'Benchmarking European Tax and Legal Environments: Indicators of Tax and Legal Environments Favouring the Development of Private Equity and Venture Capital in European Union Member States', Zaventem, Belgium (2004b).
E. Fama, 'Efficient Capital Markets II', *Journal of Finance* 46 (1991) 1575–618.
S. Feinendegen, D. Schmidt and M. Wahrenburg, 'Die Vertragsbeziehung zwischen Investoren und Venture Capital-Fonds: Eine empirische Untersuchung des europäischen Venture Capital-Marktes', Working Paper 01, Center for Financial Studies (CFS) (2002).
D. Focarelli and A. F. Pozzolo, 'The Determinants of Cross-Border Bank Shareholdings: An Analysis with Bank-Level Data from OECD Countries', Banca de Italia, Rome (1999).
B. B. Francis and I. Hasan, 'The Underpricing of Venture and Non-Venture Capital IPOs: An Empirical Investigation', *Journal of Financial Services Research* 19 (2001) 93–113.
S. A. Franzke, 'Underpricing of Venture-Backed and Non Venture-Backed IPOs: Germany's Neuer Markt', RICAFE 003, London School of Economics and Political Science (2003).
X. Freixas and J.-C. Rochet, *Microeconomics of Banking*, Cambridge: MIT Press (1998).
V. H. Fried and R. D. Hisrich, 'Toward a Model of Venture Capital Investment Decision Making', *Financial Management* 23 (1994) 28–37.
G. Gebhardt and K. M. Schmidt, 'Der Markt für Venture Capital: Anreizprobleme, Governance Strukturen und staatliche Interventionen', *Perspektiven der Wirtschaftspolitik* 3 (2002) 235–55.
S. Gifford, 'Limited Attention and the Role of the Venture Capitalist', *Journal of Business Venturing* 12 (1997) 459–82.
R. J. Gilson and D. Schizer, 'Understanding Venture Capital Structure: A Tax Explanation for Convertible Preferred Stock', Working Paper 199, Columbia Law School (2002).
R. K. Goel and I. Hasan, 'Funding New Ventures: Some Strategies for Raising Early Finance', *Applied Financial Economics* 14 (2004) 773–8.
L. Goldberg, 'When is U.S. Bank Lending to Emerging Markets Volatile?', in S. Edwards and J. Frankel (eds), *Preventing Currency Crises in Emerging Markets*, Chicago, IL: University of Chicago Press (2002).
L. Goldberg, 'The International Exposure of U.S. Banks', Working Paper 11365, National Bureau of Economic Research (NBER) (2005).
L. Goldberg, B. G. Dages and J. Crystal, 'The Lending Cycles of Banks in Emerging Markets', Federal Reserve Bank of New York, Mimeo (2002).

P. A. Gompers, 'Optimal Investment, Monitoring, and the Staging of Venture Capital', *The Journal of Finance* 50 (1995) 1461–89.

P. A. Gompers, 'Grandstanding in the Venture Capital Industry', *Journal of Financial Economics* 42 (1996) 133–56.

P. A. Gompers, 'Ownership and Control in Entrepreneurial Firms: An Examination of Convertible Securities in Venture Capital Investments', Working Paper, Harvard University, Cambridge, MA (1997).

P. A. Gompers, 'Venture Capital Growing Pains: Should the Market Diet?', *Journal of Banking and Finance* 22 (1998) 1089–104.

P. A. Gompers and J. Lerner, 'The Use of Covenants: An Empirical Analysis of Venture Partnership Agreements', *The Journal of Law and Economics* 39 (1996) 443–98.

P. A. Gompers and J. Lerner, 'The Determinants of Corporate Venture Capital Success: Organizational Structure, Incentives, and Complementarities', in R. K. Morck (ed.), *Concentrated Corporate Ownership*, Chicago: Chicago Press (1998).

P. A. Gompers and J. Lerner, *The Venture Capital Cycle*, Cambridge: MIT Press (1999a).

P. A. Gompers and J. Lerner, 'What Drives Venture Capital Fundraising?', Working Paper 6906, National Bureau of Economic Research (NBER) (1999b).

P. A. Gompers and J. Lerner, 'Money Chasing Deals? The Impact of Fund Inflows on Private Equity Valuations', *Journal of Financial Economics* 55 (2000) 281–325.

P. A. Gompers, A. Kovner, J. Lerner and D. Scharfstein, 'Venture Capital Investment Cycles: The Impact of Public Markets', Working Paper 11385, National Bureau of Economic Research (NBER) (2005).

M. Gorman and W. Sahlman, 'What Do Venture Capitalists Do?', *Journal of Business Venturing* 4 (1989) 231–48.

C. Gourieroux, A. Monfort and A. Trognon, 'Pseudo Maximum Likelihood Methods: Theory', *Econometrica* 52 (1984a) 681–700.

C. Gourieroux, A. Monfort and A. Trognon, 'Pseudo Maximum Likelihood Methods: Applications to Poisson Models', *Econometrica* 52 (1984b) 701–21.

Z. Griliches, 'The Search for R&D Spillovers', *Scandinavian Journal of Economics* 94 (1992) 29–47.

P. A. Grout, 'Investment and Wages in the Absence of Legally Binding Labor Contracts: A Nash Bargaining Approach', *Econometrica* 52 (1984) 449–60.

A. K. Gupta and H. J. Sapienza, 'Determinants of Venture Capital Firms' Preferences Regarding the Industry Diversity and Geographic Scope of their Investments', *Journal of Business Venturing* 7 (1992) 347–62.

P. Gustavson, P. Hansson and L. Lundberg, 'Technology, Resources, Endowments and International Competitiveness', *European Economic Review* 43 (1999) 1501–30.

M. Haemmig, *The Globalization of Venture Capital. A Management Study of International Capital Firms*, Bern: Verlag Paul Haupt (2003a).

M. Haemmig, 'The Globalization of Venture Capital "Israel in the International Venture Capital Arena"', *Israel Venture Capital Journal* 3 (2003b) 8–10.

F. Hardymon, J. Lerner and A. Leamon, 'Accel Partners' European Lunch', HBS Case 9-803-021, Harvard Business School, Boston, MA (2003).

D. Harhoff, 'Are there Financing Constraints for R&D Investment in German Manufacturing Firms?', *Annales D'Économie et de Statistique* 49/50 (1998) 421–56.

R. T. Harrison and C. M. Mason, 'Venture Capital Market Complementarities: The Links Between Business Angels and Venture Capital Funds in the United Kingdom', *Venture Capital: An International Journal of Entrepreneurial Finance* 2 (2000) 223–42.

J. A. Hausman, B. H. Hall and Z. Griliches, 'Econometric Models for Count Data with an Application to the Patents-R&D Relationship', *Econometrica* 52 (1984) 909–38.

U. Hege, F. Palomino and A. Schwienbacher, 'Determinants of Venture Capital Performance: Europe and the United States', RICAFE 001, London School of Economics and Political Science (2003).

T. Hellmann, L. Lindsey and M. Puri, 'Building Relationships Early: Banks in Venture Capital', Working Paper 10535, National Bureau of Economic Research (NBER) (2004).

T. Hellmann and M. Puri, 'The Interaction between Product Market and Financing Strategy: The Role of Venture Capital', *The Review of Financial Studies* 13 (2000) 959–84.

T. Hellmann and M. Puri, 'Venture Capital and the Professionalization of Start-Up Firms: Empirical Evidence', *The Journal of Finance* 57 (2002) 169–97.

C. P. Himmelberg and B. C. Petersen, 'R&D and Internal Finance: A Panel Study of Small Firms in the High-Tech Industries', *The Review of Economics and Statistics* 76 (1994) 38–51.

M. T. Holi, L. Krafft, S. Golla and H. Klandt, 'A Survey of the Venture Capital Market in Germany from 1997–2003', in A.-K. Achleitner, H. Klandt, L. T. Koch and K.-I. Voigt (eds), *Jahrbuch Entrepreneurship 2004/05*, Berlin Heidelberg: Springer Verlag (2005).

E. Houben, 'Optimale Vertragsgestaltung bei Venture-Capital-Finanzierungen', Wiesbaden: Deutscher Universitätsverlag (2006).

E. Houben and P. Nippel, 'Vertragsgestaltung bei Venture-Capital-Finanzierungen', in C. J. Börner and D. Grichnik (eds), *Entrepreneurial Finance*, Heidelberg: Physika (2005).

J. B. Hugot, *Le Guide des Sociétés de Capital-Investissement*, 3rd edition, Paris (2000).

A. Hyytinen and M. Pajarinen, 'Financial Systems and Venture Capital in Nordic Countries: A Comparative Study', in A. Hyytinen and M. Pajarinen (eds), *Financial Systems and Firm Performance. Theoretical and Empirical Perspectives*, Helsinki: Taloustieto Ltd. (2003).

A. Hyytinen and L. Väänänen, 'Government Funding of Small and Medium-Sized Enterprises in Finland', in A. Hyytinen and M. Pajarinen (eds), *Financial Systems and Firm Performance. Theoretical and Empirical Perspectives*, Helsinki: Taloustieto Ltd. (2003).

K. S. Im, M. H. Pesaran and Y. Shin, 'Testing for Unit Roots in Heterogenous Panels', *Journal of Econometrics* 115 (2003) 53–74.

IMD World Competitiveness Yearbook, Lausanne: International Institute for Management Development (IMD) (various issues).

IMF (International Monetary Fund), IFS CD-rom (International Financial Statistic) (2003).

A. B. Jaffe, 'Economic Analysis of Research Spillovers – Implications for the Advanced Technology Program', Washington: Advanced Technology Program, National Institute of Standards and Technology, U.S. Department of Commerce (1996).

L. A. Jeng and P. C. Wells, 'The Determinants of Venture Capital Funding: Evidence Across Countries', *Journal of Corporate Finance* 6 (2000) 241–89.

C. Just, *Business Angels und technologieorientierte Unternehmensgründungen-Lösungsansätze zur Behebung von Informationsdefiziten am informellen Beteiligungskapitalmarkt aus Sicht der Kapitalgeber*, Stuttgart: Fraunhofer IRB Verlag (2000).

V. Kanniainen and C. Keuschnigg, 'Start-up Investment with Scarce Venture Capital Support', *Journal of Banking & Finance* 28 (2004) 1935–59.

S. N. Kaplan and P. Strömberg, 'Financial Contracting Theory Meets the Real World: An Empirical Analysis of Venture Capital Contracts', *Review of Economic Studies* 70 (2003) 281–315.

A. K. Kashyap and J. C. Stein, 'What Do a Million Observations on Banks Say About the Transmission of Monetary Policy', *American Economic Review* 90 (2000) 407–28.

C. Keuschnigg and S. B. Nielsen, 'Public Policy for Venture Capital', *International Tax and Public Finance* 8 (2001) 557–72.

J. F. Kiviet, 'On Bias, Inconsistency and Efficiency of Various Estimators in Dynamic Panel Data Models', *Journal of Econometrics* 68 (1995) 53–78.

K. Kletzer and P. Bardhan, 'Credit Markets and Patterns in International Trade', *Journal of Development Economics* 27 (1987) 57–70.

S. Kortum and J. Lerner, 'Assessing the Contribution of Venture Capital to Innovation', *The Rand Journal of Economics* 31 (2000) 674–92.

T. Kraus, 'Underpricing of IPOs and the Certification Role of Venture Capitalists: Evidence from Germany's Neuer Markt' (2002), (February 17, 2002), http://ssrn.com/abstract=301431.

M. Kulicke, 'Innovation Networks and Regional VC Companies in Germany – Experiences for Central and Eastern European Countries', in K. Koschatzky (ed.), *Innovation Networks: Concepts and Challenges in the European Perspective*, Fraunhofer-Institut für Systemtechnik und Innovationsforschung (ISI), Heidelberg: Physica (2001).

R. La Porta, F. Lopez de Silanes, A. Shleifer and R. Vishny, 'Investor Protection and Corporate Governance', *Journal of Financial Economics* 58 (2000) 3–27.

R. Layard, S. Nickell and R. Jackman, *Unemployment, Macroeconomic Performance and the Labor Market*, Oxford: Oxford University Press (1991).

P. M. Lee and S. Wahal, 'Grandstanding, Certification and the Underpricing of Venture Capital Backed IPOs', *Journal of Financial Economics* 73 (2004) 375–407.

E. Lehmann, 'Does Venture Capital Syndication Spur Employment Growth and Shareholder Value? Evidence from German IPO Data', Diskussionspapiere 04/11, Diskussionspapiere der DFG Forschergruppe (Nr. 3468269275) (2004).

E. Lehmann and K. Boschker, *Venture Capital Syndication in Germany: Evidence from IPO Data* (2002), accessed on December 12, 2002 at http://ssrn.com/abstract=361880.

B. Leleux and B. Surlemont, 'Public versus Private Venture Capital: Seeding or Crowding Out? A Pan-European Analysis', *Journal of Business Venturing* 18 (2003) 81–104.

J. Lerner, 'The Syndication of Venture Capital Investments', *Journal of the Financial Management Association* 23 (1994a) 16–27.

J. Lerner, 'Venture Capitalists and the Decision to Go Public', *Journal of Financial Economics* 35 (1994b) 3293–316.

J. Lerner, 'Venture Capitalists and Oversight of Privately-Held Firms', *The Journal of Finance* 50 (1995) 301–18.

J. Lerner, 'When Bureaucrats Meet Entrepreneurs: The Design of Effective "Public Venture Capital" Programmes', *The Economic Journal* 112 (2002a) F73–F84.

J. Lerner, 'Boom and Bust in the Venture Capital Industry and the Impact on Innovation', Federal Reserve Bank of Atlanta Economic Review, Fourth Quarter 2002 (2002b).

V. Lessat, J. Hemer, T. Eckerle, M. Kulicke, G. Licht, E. Nerlinger, F. Steil and M. Steiger, *Beteiligungskapital und technologieorientierte Unternehmensgründungen: Markt – Finanzierung – Rahmenbedingungen*, Wiesbaden: Gabler (1999).

A. Levin, C. Lin and C. Chu, 'Unit Root Tests in Panel Data: Asymptotic and Finite Sample Properties', *Journal of Econometrics* 108 (2002) 1–24.

R. Levine and S. Zervos, 'Stock Markets, Banks, and Economic Growth', *American Economic Review* 88 (1998) 537–58.

T. H. Lin and R. L. Smith, 'Insider Reputation and Selling Decisions: The Unwinding of Venture Capital Investments during Equity IPOs', *Journal of Corporate Finance* 4 (1998) 241–63.

A. Ljungqvist and M. Richardson, 'The Investment Behaviour of Private Equity Fund Managers', RICAFE 005, London School of Economics and Political Science (2003).

A. Lockett and M. Wright, 'The Syndication of Private Equity: Evidence from the UK', *Venture Capital: An International Journal of Entrepreneurial Finance* 1 (1999) 303–24.

A. Lockett and M. Wright, 'The Syndication of Venture Capital Investments', *Omega: The International Journal of Management Science* 29 (2001) 375–90.

C. Lülfesmann, 'Start-Up Firms, Venture Capital Financing and Renegotiation', *Journal of Financial Management and Analysis* 13 (2000) 1–15.

I. C. MacMillan, D. M. Kulow and R. Khoylian, 'Venture Capitalists' Involvement in their Investments: Extent and Performance', *Journal of Business Venturing* 4 (1989) 27–47.

M. M. Mäkelä, *Essays on Cross-Border Venture Capital*, Helsinki University, Helsinki (2004).

S. Manigart, K. DeWaele, M. Wright, K. Robbie, P. Desbrières, H. J. Sapienza and A. Beekman, 'Determinants of Required Return in Venture Capital Investments: A Five-Country Study', *Journal of Business Venturing* 17 (2002) 291–312.

S. Manigart, A. Lockett, M. Meuleman, M. Wright, H. Landström, H. Bruining, P. Desbrières and U. Hommet, 'Why Do Venture Capital Companies Syndicate?', Working Paper 226, Ghent University (2004).

C. M. Mason and R. T. Harrison, 'The Geography of Venture Capital Investments in the UK', *Transactions of the Institute of British Geographers* 27 (2002) 427–51.

C. Mayer, K. Schoors and Y. Yafeh, 'Sources of Funds and Investment Activities of Venture Capital Funds: Evidence from Germany, Israel, Japan and the UK', *Journal of Corporate Finance* 11 (2005) 586–608.

W. L. Megginson and K. A. Weiss, 'Venture Capitalist Certification in Initial Public Offerings', *The Journal of Finance* 46 (1991) 879–903.

G. C. Murray and R. Marriot, 'Why has the Investment Performance of Technology-Specialist, European Venture Capital Funds been so Poor?', *Research Policy* 27 (1998) 947–76.

W. Neus and U. Walz, 'Exit Timing of Venture Capitalists in the Course of an Initial Public Offering', *Journal of Financial Intermediation* 14 (2005) 253–77.

S. Nickell, 'Biases in Dynamic Models with Fixed Effects', *Econometrica* 49 (1981) 1417–26.

E. Norton and B. H. Tenenbaum, 'Specialization versus Diversification as a Venture Capital Investment Strategy', *Journal of Business Venturing* 8 (1993) 431–42.

NVCA (National Venture Capital Association), NVCA Yearbook, Arlington, VA. (2004).

OECD (Organization for Economic Co-Operation and Development), Government Venture Capital for Technology-Based Firms, OECD/GD(97)201, Paris (1997).

OECD (Organization for Economic Co-Operation and Development), 'OECD Employment Outlook' (1999).

OECD (Organization for Economic Co-Operation and Development), Risk Capital in OECD Countries: Recent Developments and Structural Issues. Financial Market Trends 82, June, OECD (2002a).

OECD (Organization for Economic Co-Operation and Development), Entrepreneurship and Growth: Tax Issues. Directorate for Science, Technology and Industry Paris (2002b).

OECD (Organization for Economic Co-Operation and Development), Institutional Investor Database 2003 (2003a).

OECD (Organization for Economic Co-Operation and Development), 'OECD Bank Profitability Statistics' (2003b).

OECD (Organization for Economic Co-Operation and Development), 'OECD Main Science and Technology Statistics' (2003c).

OECD (Organization for Economic Co-Operation and Development), 'OECD Statistical Compendium' (2004).

OECD (Organization for Economic Co-Operation and Development), 'OECD STAN database for industrial analysis' (various issues).

O. Pfirrmann, U. Wupperfeld and J. Lerner, *Venture Capital and New Technology Based Firms: A US-German Comparison*, Heidelberg: Physica (1997).

R. Portes and H. Rey, 'The Determinants of Cross-Border Equity Flows', Working Paper 7336, National Bureau of Economic Research (NBER) (1999).

J. M. Poterba, 'Venture Capital and Capital Gain Taxation', *Tax Policy and the Economy* 3 (1989) 47–67.

R. G. Rajan and L. Zingales, 'Financial Dependence and Growth', *American Economic Review* 88 (1998) 559–86.

R. Repullo and J. Suarez, 'Venture Capital Finance: A Security Design Approach', *Review of Finance* 8 (2004) 75–108.

G. Rindermann, 'Venture Capitalist Participation and the Performance of IPO Firms: Empirical Evidence from France, Germany and the UK', EFMA 2003 Helsinki Meetings, http://ssrn.com/abstract=425080.

Y. E. Riyanto and A. Schwienbacher, 'On the Strategic Use of Corporate Venture Financing for Securing Demand', Working Paper 109, National University of Singapore (2002).

E. B. Rock, 'Greenhorns, Yankees and Cosmopolitans: Venture Capital, IPOs, Foreign Firms and U.S. Markets', Research Paper 01–07, University of Pennsylvania Law School (2001).

E. B. Rock, 'Coming to America? Venture Capital, Corporate Identity and U.S. Securities Law', Research Paper 02–07, University of Pennsylvania Law School (2002).

A. Romain and B. van Pottelsberghe, 'The Determinants of Venture Capital: Additional Evidence', Discussion Paper Series 1: Studies of the Economic Research Centre 19, Deutsche Bundesbank (2004).

J. C. Ruhnka and J. E. Young, 'A Venture Capital Model of the Development Process for New Ventures', *Journal of Business Venturing* 2 (1987) 167–84.

J. C. Ruhnka and J. E. Young, 'Some Hypotheses about Risk in Venture Capital Investing', *Journal of Business Venturing* 6 (1991) 115–33.

W. A. Sahlman, 'The Structure and Governance of Venture-Capital Organizations', *Journal of Financial Economics* 27 (1990) 473–521.

H. Sapienza, 'When Do Venture Capitalists Add Value?', *Journal of Business Venturing* 7 (1992) 9–27.

H. Sapienza, S. Manigart and W. Vermeir, 'Venture Capitalist Governance and Value-Added in Four Countries', *Journal of Business Venturing* 11 (1996) 439–70.

A. Schertler, 'A Comparative Overview of Venture Capital in Europe and the United States', *International Journal of Entrepreneurship Education* 1 (2002/2003).

A. Schertler, *Dynamic Efficiency and Path Dependencies in Venture Capital Markets*, Berlin: Springer (2003).

A. Schertler, 'Explaining Cross-Country Variations in Venture Capital Investments: Theory and Empirical Evidence', *Kredit & Kapital* 37 (2004) 297–328.

A. Schertler, 'European Venture Capital Markets: Fund Providers and Investment Characteristics', *Applied Financial Economics* 15 (2005a) 367–80.

A. Schertler, 'Knowledge Capital and Venture Capital Investments: New Evidence from European Panel Data', *German Economic Review* (forthcoming) (2005b).

K. M. Schmidt, 'Convertible Securities and Venture Capital Finance', *The Journal of Finance* 58 (2003) 1139–66.

D. Schmidt and M. Wahrenburg, 'Contractual Relations between European VC–Funds and Investors: The Impact of Reputation and Bargaining Power on Contractual Design', Working Paper 15, Center for Financial Studies (CFS) (2003).

K. Schween, *Corporate Venture Capital: Risikokapitalfinanzierung deutscher Industrieunternehmen*, Wiesbaden: Gabler (1996).

A. Schwienbacher, 'An Empirical Analysis of Venture Capital Exits in Europe and in the United States', University of Namur (2002).

S. B. Smart and C. J. Zutter, 'Control as a Motivation for Underpricing: A Comparison of Dual- and Single-Class IPOs', *Journal of Financial Economics* 69 (2000) 85–110.

D. G. Smith, 'Team Production in Venture Capital Investing', *Journal of Corporation Law* 25 (1999).

P. Smith, 'Transatlantic Misalignment in Fund-Raising', *Financial Times* April 21, 2004, Nr. 35433, London (2004a) p. 17.

P. Smith, 'Groups Use IPOs to Fund Opportunities: Private Equity Companies Use Public Markets in Hunt for New Capital', *Financial Times* April 19, 2004, Nr. 35431, London (2004b) p. 19.

O. Sorenson and T. E. Stuart, 'Syndication Networks and the Spatial Distribution of Venture Capital Investments', *American Journal of Sociology* 106 (2002) 1546–88.

M. Stolpe, 'Learning and Signaling in the French and German Venture Capital Industries', Working Paper 1156, Kiel Institute for World Economics (2003).

H. Svaleryd and J. Vlachos, 'Financial Markets, the Pattern of Industrial Specialization and Comparative Advantage: Evidence from OECD Countries', *European Economic Review* 49 (2005) 113–44.

R. Tejada, 'Venture Capital Policy Review: Spain. STI Working Paper 18, Industry Issues', Organization for Economic Co-operation and Development (OECD) (2003a).

R. Tejada, 'Venture Capital Policy Review: Portugal. STI Working Paper 19, Industry Issues', Organization for Economic Co-operation and Development (OECD) (2003b).

E. Theissen, 'Organized Equity Markets in Germany', Working Paper 17, Center for Financial Studies (CFS) (2003).

T. Tykvova, 'Who are the True Venture Capitalists in Germany?', Discussion Paper 04–16, Zentrum für Europäische Wirtschaftsforschung GmbH (ZEW) (2004).

T. Tykvova and U. Walz, 'Are IPOs of Different VCs Different?', Discussion Paper 04–32, Zentrum für Europäische Wirtschaftsforschung GmbH (ZEW) (2004).

M. Ueda, 'Banks versus Venture Capital: Project Evaluation, Screening, and Expropriation', *The Journal of Finance* 53 (2004) 601–21.

M. Van Osnabrugge and R. J. Robinson, *Angel Investing, Matching Start-up Funds with Start-up Companies*, San Francisco: Jossey-Bass (2000).

VentureCapital Magazin 9/2003, 'Die Private Equity-Tabelle des Monats: EVCA erforscht Europas Dachfonds-Landschaft', Wolfratshausen (2003) p. 29.

N. Wasserman, 'Building to a Crescendo', HBS case N1–804–009, Harvard Business School, Boston, MA (2003).

P. Weimerskirch, *Finanzierungsdesign bei Venture-Capital-Verträgen*, Wiesbaden: Deutscher Universitätsverlag (1998).

R. Wilson, 'The Theory of Syndicates', *Econometrica* 36 (1968) 119–32.

F. Windmeijer, 'A Finite Sample Correction for the Variance of Linear Two-Step GMM Estimators', *Journal of Econometrics* 126 (2005) 25–51.

J. M. Wooldridge, *Econometric Analysis of Cross-Section and Panel Data*, Cambridge, MA: MIT Press (2002).

M. Wright and A. Lockett, 'The Structure and Management of Alliances: Syndication in the Venture Capital Industry', *Journal of Management Studies* 40 (2003) 2073–104.

M. Wright, A. Lockett and S. Pruthi, 'Internationalization of Western Venture Capitalists into Emerging Markets: Risk Assessment and Information in India', *Small Business Economics* 19 (2002) 13–29.

M. Wright and K. Robbie, 'Venture Capital and Private Equity: A Review and Synthesis', *Journal of Business Finance and Accounting* 25 (1998) 521–71.

U. Wupperfeld, 'Die Betreuung junger Technologieunternehmen durch ihre Beteiligungskapitalgeber. Empirische Untersuchung', Working Paper, Institut für Systemtechnik und Innovationsforschung (ISI), Karlsruhe (1994).

I. Zemke, *Die Unternehmensverfassung von Beteiligungskapital-Gesellschaften. Analyse des institutionellen Designs deutscher Venture Capital-Gesellschaften*, Wiesbaden: Gabler (1995).

Index

Printed and bound by CPI Group (UK) Ltd, Croydon, CR0 4YY